What's Going on Here?

US experiences of Islamophobia between Obama and Trump

Saied R. Ameli and Saeed A. Khan

Islamic Human Rights Commission

www.ihrc.org.uk

First published in the United Kingdom in 2020
by Islamic Human Rights Commission
PO Box 598, Wembley, HA9 7XH
Copyright © Islamic Human Rights Commission, 2020

Typeset by Ibrahim Sadikovic
Cover image: Noor Hindi (left) and Sham Najjar, born in the US
of Syrian parents, demonstrating against the US immigration ban
at the Los Angeles International Airport on January 30, 2017.
Photo Mark Ralston, AFP/Getty Images

ISBN 978-1-909853-10-2

Printed by Mega Printing in Turkey

Contents

List of Tables:

List of Graphs:

Acknowledgments

From Saied R. Ameli: I would like to acknowledge and thank the immense contribution of Ebrahim Mohseni Ahooei in the data analysis in this volume.

From Saeed Khan: I would like to extend my appreciation and gratitude to IHRC for providing the vision, support and opportunity to be part of this project, especially to Arzu Merali and Massoud Shadjareh for all that they do and inspire.

Thank you to my home institution, Wayne State University, and my colleagues there for creating the atmosphere that allows me to be the proverbial kid in an intellectual candy store. Also, thanks to my students- past, present and future. You recharge my quest for knowledge and passion for teaching every single day.

Lastly, my humble thanks to my family and friends. For fear of forgetting any of them, and to protect their privacy for being associated with me and to save several pages of print, I won't name each one. But you know who you are; and in my life, I love you more.

IHRC wishes to thank Lena Mohamed for her indefatigable work in making this research a reality, Ashiya Mendheria for her hard work and support, and Adam Majeed and Faisal Bodi for their attention to detail.

Chapter 1

Origins of Islam in America

The history of Islam in America predates the establishment of the country by nearly 800 years. There is now scholarly evidence that Muslim explorers discovered the Americas during the reign of Abd Ar-Rahman III of Cordoba in the early to mid 10th century. During the Columbian explorations of the Americas, it is now known that two of Columbus's three ships on his initial expedition were captained by Muslims, the brothers Martin Alonso Pinzon aboard the Pinta and Vicente Yáñez Pinzón aboard the Nina. Muslim cartographers and navigators also comprised part of this late 15th century European endeavour. The maps that doubtless were consulted regarding the maritime routes had been drafted by Muslims. (GhaneaBassiri, 2010) Muslims also played a role in exploring territory deep within the continental United States on behalf of the Spanish empire. For example, Estevanico of Azamor explored Arizona and New Mexico during the 1520s and 1530s (Herrick, 2018).

Of course, the first identifiable influx of Muslims to the Americas came by way of the Atlantic slave trade. Estimates place as much as 30% of American slaves having been of Muslim heritage. The deracination of Islam from these Muslims was a function of stripping them of their identity, their culture and their dignity. The process of Christianization was also under the aegis of the so-called "White Man's Burden" of civilizing the purported "savage man." (GhaneaBassiri, 2010) This despite the fact that West African Islamic culture was vibrant, refined and prosperous. There is the case, for example, of Ayuba Suleyman Diallo, from Bundu, Senegal, also known as the noble slave. He was taken into slavery, despite being from a prominent west African family, in 1731. His name was Anglicized to become Job Ben Solomon. He is said to have astonished his slave masters by his ability to write in Arabic, as well as his transcription of three copies of the Qur'an, strictly from memory (Smith, 1999).

Muslims played a role in the establishment of the United States from its earliest stages. During the American revolutionary war, Muslims fought in General George Washington's Continental Army. Bampett Muhammad fought on the Virginia Line, from 1775-1778. Yusuf Ben Ali was also a soldier for the American forces, and Peter Buckminster Salem was responsible for killing British Major General John Pitcairn at the Battle of

Bunker Hill in 1775, one of the earliest military engagements in the War of Independence (Curtis, 2010).

It is also important to note that the very first country to recognize a nascent United States was Morocco. Muhammad Ben Abdullah, the Sultan of Morocco, wrote a letter to Benjamin Franklin the US Minister to France in 1777, seeking diplomatic relations and formally recognizing American independence. In 1786, Ben Abdallah signed the Moroccan American Treaty of Friendship with Thomas Jefferson and John Adams. It still remains the longest unbroken treaty between the United States and another country. Muslims also fought in the Union Army during the American Civil War between 1861 to 1865 (GhaneaBassiri, 2010).

Restrictive immigration policy limited the number of immigrants from entering the United States. Many of the countries and regions targeted by such ethnically and racially-based prohibitions included Muslim lands. The 1891 Immigration Act barred people who believed in polygamy. Between 1909 and 1917, 73 of 2457 Indians were barred from entry to the United States under these terms. One such individual, move the Mohamed Sadiq, an Ahmadi, was detained for belonging "to a religion that sanctioned polygamy." (GhaneaBassiri, 2010)

One of the first Muslim immigrants of identifiable renown came to the United States in 1923. Hazrat Inayat Khan was a Sufi musician from India, who preached a spiritual message of pluralism. Upon his arrival, Khan was detained by Ellis Island immigration officials because the quota of Indians had been completed a month earlier. Khan was eventually able to gain entry by dissociating his message of pluralism from Islam due to the awareness of anti-Islam sentiments that prevailed in the United States at the time (GhaneaBassiri, 2010). The negative perception of Islam in the beginning of the 20th century was caused by World War I and the perception of Turks and Syrians in particular being enemies of the triple entente. Some antipathy toward Turks had been fueled by the history of the Greek independence movement from 1821 to 1829 and the Armenian purge of 1915.

The mapping of the Muslim community in America gained some morphology in the early 20th century. Research conducted by M. M. Aigian, an Armenian American missionary for Muslim immigrants in Chicago, estimates that between 10 to 15% of immigrants to the United States between the years 1890 and 1924 were Muslim. (GhaneaBassiri, 2010) Due to American immigration policy at the time, it is difficult to accurately assess the religious affiliation of these immigrants especially as many came from lands in the Ottoman Empire, where religious diversity was rife. Immigration officials would usually document the region of origin, rather than any particular religious or even ethnic category.

While considered a heretical and cultish sect in British India, the Ahmadiyya movement was one of the earliest and most successful missionary programs in America. Founded in the late 19th century in what is today northern Pakistan, and treated as pariahs there, the Ahmadiyya migrants channeled their energies in spreading their message overseas. They were responsible for facilitating the earliest engagements between African Americans and the wave of Muslim migrants in the early 20th century. In 1921, for example, Mohammad Sadiq established the Ahmadiyya Muslim Community's headquarters and the Wabash (Al Sadiq) Mosque the following year, both in Chicago.

By 1920, the Muslim population in the United States was estimated to be "in the thousands." Many were concentrated in the industrial centers of the Northeast including in New York, Philadelphia, Baltimore, Boston and Worcester Massachusetts, as well as the Midwest, in places like Cleveland, Akron and Toledo, Ohio, Detroit and Flint, Michigan, Gary, Indiana, Milwaukee, Wisconsin and Chicago. There was an identifiable Muslim community, consisting of an estimated 150 Syrian families, in Ross, North Dakota in the 1920s. One of the country's earliest mosques and dedicated Muslim cemeteries is there, although the oldest standing mosque still in use is in Cedar Rapids, Iowa, established in 1934. By 1926, the United States had an estimated Muslim population of 50 to 60,000. According to research conducted by Mary Caroline Holmes, a missionary, these Muslims were growing in number in the Northeast and Midwest major urban areas but had also reached other cities such as St. Louis, San Francisco and Los Angeles. According to the 1930 US census, the United States had 10,457 Turkish speakers. This influx coincided with the fall of the Ottoman Empire after

World War I. It is assumed that many of these immigrants were in fact Muslim. Bosnian Muslims made their way as common laborers to Chicago and Gary, Indiana, to serve as diggers for the Chicago Subway system. They also were employed as copper miners in Butte, Montana. According to the 1920 census the Albanian population in the United States was 5515. Within a decade, that number grew to 8,814. By 1939, there were an estimated 35,000 to 60,000 Albanian Muslims in America (GhaneaBassiri, 2010). The Albanian Muslim community in Detroit, for example, has had a presence since 1940. Like Muslims from the Levant, Albanian Muslims flocked to Detroit to work in the assembly lines of automobile companies like Ford. Its founder, Henry Ford, actively recruited labor from the former Ottoman Empire and helped turn metropolitan Detroit into a Muslim hub as well as enclaves like Dearborn into the largest concentration of Arabs outside the Middle East.

Levantine immigration was facilitated by American missionaries who favored Arab Christians over Muslims from the region. Some Muslims migrated through the technique of "de-Islamicization" whereby they took on Christian names as a means to escape the stigma of being Turkish and or Muslim. The National Origins Act of 1924 favored immigration from northern and western European countries. It in fact excluded entry of Asians and other nonwhites. This legislation severely affected Muslim sending regions, reducing annual immigration from 358,000 to 164,000. The Asiatic exclusion league lobbied for restrictions on "Orientals" who were defined as East Asians and Indians. The law was finally abolished by the US Congress in the 1960s. (GhaneaBassiri, 2010)

Satti Majid was a self-proclaimed representative of Islam. A Sudanese missionary, Majid was responsible for establishing several organizations in the United States, including the Islamic Benevolence Society in Detroit. He also initiated the Detroit chapter of the Red Crescent and purchased plots for Muslim burial in the city's Roselawn Cemetery. Majid was responsible for converting many African Americans in Pittsburgh to Islam and may have influenced Noble Drew Ali, the founder of the Moorish Science Temple (GhaneaBassiri, 2010).

The diversity that would eventually come to describe and define the Muslim American community was reflected by the variety of ethnic and vocational demographics among those who migrated to the United States in the early 20th century. It was a collection that included students and merchants, as well as sailors. Not everyone was "above deck," so to speak; some came as stowaways. Without much surprise, these Muslims used the same migration routes across the Atlantic as were being employed by the deluge of immigrants coming from western and eastern Europe at the time. The East Coast of the United States was the first port of entry for Muslims as well, be it the famed Ellis Island in New York Harbour, or other cities like Boston, Philadelphia and Baltimore, all possessing thriving seaports.

The early influx of Muslim immigrants in the 20th century organized as communities based on ethnicity or national origin where they could find a critical mass existing in such capacities. This was not always easy as such communities were still in their embryonic stages of growth. As a result, intermarriage was also a common reality. An example of this form of social interaction concerns Fazal Khan, who migrated from British India in 1912. Khan met and married an African-American woman, and started a family somewhere on the Atlantic coast of America. One of their children, a daughter named Lurey Khan, is the common ancestor for several descendants of Fazal Khan and his intermarriage. An examination of marriage records from the early 20th century confirms that Fazal Khan's story was one of many such unions that occurred between Muslim immigrants and particularly members of the African-American community in several eastern states including Delaware, Maryland, New Jersey, New York and Pennsylvania. (GhaneaBassiri, 2010) For many of these relationships, the dearth of viable options often created the opportunities for intermarriage; in effect, the challenge of finding members of one's own ethnic or religious community, coupled with the desire to enter domestic life and begin a family were compelling enough reasons to marry across racial and religious lines.

The impetus for family life was not the only compelling reason for Muslim immigrants to consider when entering into a marriage. Given the nascent nature of the community and its relative unfamiliarity with the American social landscape, institution building was a priority for some new arrivals. Shaykh

Daoud Faisal was the son of a Grenadine (West Indian) mother and a Moroccan immigrant father, while his wife, Khadija, had a "Pakistani" (pre-partition western India) father and a mother who, like Faisal, was Black Caribbean. Together, Shaykh Daoud and Khadija founded the Islamic Mission of America. (GhaneaBassiri, 2010)

The Moorish Science Temple was one of the earliest established Muslim institutions in the United States. While the brainchild of Noble Drew Ali, it was a space that certainly highlighted the intersection between the respective African American Muslim and immigrant Muslim experiences. In the 1930s, the Ahmadiyyah movement made significant inroads into the vanguard of the American Muslim scene. Deemed a heretical and cultish sect in British India, the Ahmadiyyah were pioneers in Islamic missionary work in the United States. Yusuf Khan, an Ahmadi from India, arrived in Pittsburgh, at the First Muslim Mosque of Pittsburgh, a Moorish Science Temple from its foundation. Khan was shocked to discover that most of the congregants had no knowledge or even experience of a Qur'an, and he embarked upon teaching them the fundamental tenets of Islam. Unfortunately, tensions developed when congregants began to disagree with Khan's teachings, which did not align with those espoused by the Moorish Science Temple. One of the key areas of discord was on the Temple's focus on black nationalism, whereas Khan was arguing that Islam did not profess racial or nationalistic ideas. Another area of contention emerged in 1935, when congregants became averse to Khan's Ahmadiyyah beliefs as being inimical to their own perspectives on Islam. It is interesting to see the shift in the Temple attendees' views toward Khan as it suggests they were starting to come into contact with a more diverse group of Muslim immigrants, particularly Sunni Muslims who would have doubtless expressed their criticism of the Ahmadiyyah movement and branded it a heresy. Ironically, those same Sunni Muslims had serious issues with the belief system of the Moorish Science Temple itself. They felt that Noble Drew Ali had in fact devised a different Qur'an, "the Holy Koran." They contended that it was a blasphemy to alter divine scripture and to create something that dramatically deviated from the original Qur'an. Noble Drew Ali's assertion that God was in fact black also vexed the Sunni

Muslims, for whom the very notion of God having human attributes like race was utterly abhorrent, if not blasphemous. (Smith 1999)

There is no doubt that African American Islam was a powerful and influential movement in the United States when it entered the public sphere in the 1920s. The Nation of Islam and the Moorish Science Temple were primarily imperatives established to counter the overwhelming dominance and racially biased White Anglo-Saxon Protestant hegemon, whose victory after the First World War further emboldened its sense of racial superiority. The African American expression of Islam, as represented by NOI and MST, allowed for an empowering faith tradition, of their own agency, that allowed for the assertion of a unique identity distinct from the institutions developed by "White America." This powerful counternarrative from within a theological discourse enjoyed the protections granted by the Constitution for religious organizations under the First Amendment. In addition, African American Islam was deployed as a political vehicle for a group of Americans who were voiceless or poorly represented within the existing political architecture of the country. (Curtis, 2013)

World War II proved to be a catalyst for a paradigm shift in American national identity. There was a deviation from the white Anglo-Saxon essentialism that had defined the nation since its inception. This was due in part to the large numbers of non-white Anglo-Saxon Protestants who fought and died during the war. This indigenization effect was a function of a multi-ethnic, multi religious armed forces that defended the nation and its security irrespective of the racial composition of the fighting military. A second key factor in the postwar era that help to recalibrate America's identity was the 1954 US Supreme Court decision in *Brown vs Board of Education*, which ended a nearly centuries' old policy of segregation of the national school system. At the same time the postwar era was still marked with severe civil rights discrepancies and institutionalized racism and discrimination, particularly against African-Americans. African-American Muslims were at the vanguard of resistance to unjust, racial policies. The Nation of Islam and Moorish Science Temple members refused to register for selective service during the 1950s and the 1960s. This government policy to register all able-bodied males for the military draft was opposed by the two organizations who deemed military intervention during the Cold War as simply being "the white man's war." It is important to note however, that government actions particularly toward the African-American community were racially and politically, not religiously motivated. As such, government actions to enforce the selective service system and prosecutions against those in noncompliance of it did not discriminate between African American Muslims and non-Muslims. The Nation of Islam declared its opposition to the draft claiming that this policy violated the laws of Allah. Part of its rationale was predicated on the reality that many of the conflicts in which the United States was deploying its military forces were occurring in lands that included significant Muslim populations, such as South Asia, Southeast Asia, the Middle East and Africa. (Curtis, 2013)

New Muslim organizations started to emerge in the 1950s in the United States as a result of increasing migration and the demand to address new and rising needs for this community. The Federation of Islamic Associations (FIA) became the primary American organization for Muslim immigrants during the 1950s and 1960s. Abdullah Igram, a former officer during World War II and second generation Muslim American, established the FIA in 1952. The FIA's former name was the International Muslim Society; the FIA organized its first annual convention, drawing Muslims from across the country as well as Canada, in Cedar Rapids, Iowa (GhaneaBassiri, 2010). As would be expected from an umbrella group, the FIA's conventions and events mostly satisfied the important objective of developing a sense of community and affirming Muslim identity among the immigrant population. Although the target audience was first and second generation immigrant Muslim Americans, several African American Muslims also took part in FIA gatherings as members and attendees.

At a time in American history when patriotism and loyalty were being framed as critical criteria to prove one's allegiance to the nation, in the midst of Cold War geopolitics and the perceived threat of communism, opposition to the military draft and even dissent to the propriety of American military interventions overseas were seen as subversive acts and potential threats to national security. While many began to oppose the draft and in particular American intervention in the Vietnam conflict during the mid to late 1960s, it took the act of one prominent African American Muslim to highlight in the most visible manner US policy and the exercise of American citizenship to oppose improper and arguably illegal policy. Muhammad Ali, the world heavyweight boxing champion had begun his spiritual journey within the Nation of Islam in the early 1960s. An acolyte of both Elijah Mohammed and Malcolm X, Muhammad Ali shed his prior name, Cassius Marcellus Clay in favor of his new Islamic identity. His decision to oppose the draft on the grounds of being a conscientious objector cost him three years in the prime of his athletic career. Ali was stripped of his titles and stripped of his license to box professionally. As opposition to the draft was a criminal act, Ali was subsequently prosecuted. He fought his conviction all the way to the US Supreme Court, and in the process changed US constitutional law forever. (Curtis, 2013) His principled stance was based both on his religious convictions as well as his empathy and solidarity for people of colour across the world who were targets and pawns in the perpetual clash of the superpowers during the Cold War. Of course, Ali had more than his fair share of detractors within American civil society. It is hardly a coincidence that many of his harshest critics attributed his purported disloyalty as being a function of his race and religion. This perceived lack of allegiance and heresy to American jingoism was framed as a justification for religious and racial bigotry. Eventually, Ali's return to the boxing ring and subsequent successes – reclaiming the heavyweight title, along with his status as a beloved global cultural icon and goodwill ambassador for America - allowed him to transcend the blatant racism that he endured both prior to and during his legal challenges.

The Immigration and Nationality Act of 1965 completely changed the quotas for migration to the United States from non-European countries and in the process changed the demographic complexion of the nation for good. (United States, 1980) Coinciding with the enactment of the Civil Rights Act of 1964, the new immigration law significantly relaxed quotas for migrants from Asia and Africa. This resulted in a massive influx of immigrants from both continents including Muslim majority countries in South Asia, the Middle East, South East Asia and North and sub-Saharan Africa. One indicator of the impact of this change in legislation was the increase in Muslim foreign students. In 1948 they numbered 2,708, a number which swelled to 13,664 by 1965. While Muslim immigrants arrived in the United States representing myriad countries and vocations, the immigration laws favored and facilitated entry for those applicants who came from technical and professional career trajectories. (GhaneaBissari, 2010)

The Muslim Student Association (MSA), established in 1963, was intended to be a network for Muslim foreign students obtaining higher education in the United States. It was envisaged to provide religious services and resources, as well as to furnish students with the reinforcement of their sense of Muslim identity as many were thousands of miles away from their respective homes. (www.msanational.org) While it may be inferred that many of the MSA's early membership intended to return to their respective home countries upon completion of their education programs, many stayed in the United States upon obtaining their degrees and credentials. Economic opportunity in America as well as political volatility in their respective home countries served as compelling factors of consideration for their decision to remain in the United States. Given their choice to establish roots within the country, the founders of the MSA recognized the need of establishing a new organization which could meet the needs for the post graduate Muslim community. As a result, the Islamic Society of North America was founded. While initially a subgroup of the MSA, ISNA acquired its own independent status as an institution in 1982. Its headquarters was strategically located in Plainfield Indiana, symbolically in the heartland of America's Midwest, close to the University of Illinois, home to the first MSA, and Chicago, with its growing Muslim community. ISNA then went on to create a youth based affiliate, the Muslim Youth of North America (MYNA) as a pre-MSA organization designed for young Muslims at primary and secondary school levels. (www.isna.net)

Some of the initial Muslim organizations formed by immigrant groups were predominantly nationalist and secular in their focus and ideology. In part, this was due to the simple fact that American sociological modalities in the early to mid 20th century were by and large a function of racial distinctions than forged along religious lines. While there was certainly discrimination against Catholics and Jews in those years, much of the discrimination was framed in terms of ethnicity and race. Catholics arrived in the United States primarily from countries like Ireland and Italy; they were perceived, until the post-World War II era, as being non-white, as were others from southern and eastern Europe, which included Slavs and Jews. As such, and given the obvious outward foreign-ness of Islam in the public imagination as well as the secularity of civil society, Muslim immigrants tended to focus on cultural identity over religious affiliation. Organizations such as the Free Syria Society and the New Syria Party reflected the consciousness of Syrian Arabs coping with the considerable transformation of their homeland during the interwar period, with the advent of the Mandate System. These organizations had a diverse membership of the various religious groups that comprised Syrian society, as national identity allowed for inclusion of the largest possible contingent and also had the equally important consequence of keeping religious difference at a distance, given the divisive confessional politics of the home country (Bawardi, 2014).

The increased influx of immigrant Muslims starting in the 1960s created a more visible and reoriented focus on Muslim identity as a religious-cultural category. It also reflected the changing priorities for the American Muslim community that had begun to form roots and a sense of rootedness in the United States. With consideration for their futures as well as those of their progeny, Muslim American immigrants embarked upon an ambitious project of building mosques in major Muslim population centers throughout the 1970s and 1980s. By the end of the 20th century, an estimated 2,500 mosques dotted the American landscape, with dozens more being established each year. As would be expected, the vast majority of these centers are located in large Muslim areas, like New York, Chicago, Detroit, Philadelphia, Atlanta, Houston. Dallas, Los Angeles and the San Francisco Bay Area. (Bagby, 2001)

Islamic education began as a gradual initiative to teach young Muslim Americans the basics of the faith, including the Qur'an, prophetic tradition and fundamental rules of liturgy and observance. Often, these programs would be weekend "schools" similar to the time-honoured American Sunday school. A push for more permanent and established curricular schools occurred as community resources allowed, especially beginning in the 1980s Today, the United States has hundreds of "Islamic" schools that offer a full kindergarten to 12th grade curriculum, and operate like Catholic or other religious-affiliated schools. (Khan, 2017) In addition, programs that offer memorization of the Qur'an (Hifz) and even Muslim seminaries have developed in various Muslim communities. The Muslim American community also has two dedicated Islamic universities. The American Islamic College in Chicago was established in 1983, (www.aicusa.edu) while Zaytuna College was founded in Berkeley, California in the year 2008. (zaytuna.edu)

Beyond mosques and Islamic schools, many Muslim American organizations were established as a response to specific needs facing the community over the preceding few decades. The Council on American Islamic Relations (CAIR) was founded after 1994 as an advocacy and civil rights organization to address the needs of Muslim Americans in the aftermath of the 1993 World Trade Center attack. CAIR has multiple regional chapters across the country and serves to provide legal representation and advocacy of Muslim rights. Similarly, Muslim Advocates was founded after the passage of the USA Patriot Act in 2001 as an organization dedicated to the advocacy of Muslim Americans in their pursuit to combat bigotry. The Muslim Public Affairs Council (MPAC) was created in 1986 to serve as a public policy and advocacy organization for Muslim Americans. It focuses heavily on promoting and correcting the narrative about Muslim Americans both within the political arena of Washington DC and state political spaces, as well as media and entertainment depiction of Muslims and Islam. (Love, 2017)

The 9-11 attacks exposed the deficiencies within the Muslim American organizational network. The aftermath of the terrorist acts and the ensuing backlash faced by the community created new opportunities for new initiatives that would help complete necessary areas of Muslim American civic and political engagement. In 2001, the Institute for Social Policy and Understanding (ISPU) was founded in Detroit as a think tank, focusing on American social and domestic policy from a Muslim American perspective. To date, ISPU remains at the forefront of providing scholarly and accurate data about the Muslim American community, its perspectives and its issues. In addition, other post 911 organizations have emerged, facilitated by the Internet and social media, to provide a host of Islamic knowledge to Muslim Americans of all ages. (www.ispu.org) Such organizations include the Yaqeen Institute, Bayyinah Institute and Al Medina Institute.

US State Policy vis-à-vis Muslims

American policy toward the so-called Muslim world since the end of World War II has primarily been a function of two geopolitical and strategic priorities. Initially, the Cold War required the United States to position client states to prevent the expansion of Soviet/communist influence, particularly in areas of American hegemony. The second and related impetus centered on American efforts to dominate the petroleum industry. Before the conclusion of World War II, then President Franklin Delano Roosevelt sought to confirm American relations with Saudi Arabia and its burgeoning oil sector. Roosevelt met with King Abdulaziz Al Saud in 1945 after attending the Yalta conference with Winston Churchill and Joseph Stalin. A mere few weeks before his death, Roosevelt wanted to assert the strategic alliance between Washington and Riyadh that was essential for America's international position in the postwar era. (Bronson, 2008) As critical as it was for the United States to create barriers to Soviet expansion, Washington also sought to place curbs on the imperial ambitions of its own purported allies, the British and the French. The United States implemented significant measures to combat the prospect of Soviet influence expanding to the Middle East. Under the guise of containing communism, the United States entered into the so-called Baghdad Pact, also known as the Central Treaty Organization, or CENTO, in 1955. This mutual defense treaty, similar to NATO, involved the United States, Great Britain, and four Muslim countries: Iran, Iraq, Pakistan and Turkey. Given its geostrategic location, Turkey was and is a member of the NATO alliance as well, the only Muslim country to be included within that group. (Sayigh, 2003) America's zealous obsession with countering Soviet influence resulted in US policy overlooking, ignoring, and in some cases willfully preventing the establishment and spread of democracy in Muslim countries. For the United States, the fallacy of stability brought about by dictatorships was far more palatable than the perceived benefits and fluidity of democratic states. While no such concession or ethical quagmire existed for Western European nations, Washington made certain that its geostrategic interests and priorities took precedence at the expense of the well-being, human rights, political wellbeing and self-determination of millions living in regimes that served the purposes of American foreign policy.

Countries whose leaders are suspected of equivocating on their commitment to categorical subordination to American policy objectives faced the prospect of an overthrow of government. The classic example of the intersection of Cold War politics and petro-politics was the infamous 1953 CIA orchestrated overthrow of a democratically elected Prime Minister Mohamed Mossadegh in Iran. Upon his election in 1951, Mossadegh sought to implement the 1950 Iran Nationalization Act, which took control of the country's oil sector from the British. Despite being fully within the auspices of international law, American and British authorities would not countenance a sovereign state having control over its own national assets. Mossadegh's overthrow coincided with the resumption of full despotic rule by the last Shah of Iran, Muhammad Reza Pahlavi. The Shah also positioned himself as a reliable, staunchly anti-communist ally to Washington and in return, was granted the proverbial green light to procure any and all means to maintain power, even if it meant the suppression of his own people. Until his abdication in 1979, in the midst of the Iranian Revolution, the Shah was one of America's most reliable allies in the Middle East, with Saudi Arabia, one of the so-called twin pillars of US foreign policy in the Persian Gulf. Washington authorized the sale of any non-nuclear munitions in the American arsenal to Tehran. Of course, such categorical support for the Shah and complicity in his campaign of suppression set the stage for the antagonistic relationship that developed after the Revolution and that persists to the present time. (Kinzer, 2003)

American policy decisions in the midst of the 1979 Iranian Revolution forged the crucible in which Washington-Tehran relations would be conducted henceforth. While the Iranians were justifiably aggrieved at American support for the Shah and his policies of oppression, the new regime led by Ayatollah Khomeini initially maintained an ambivalent attitude toward Washington. Unfortunately, American obstinacy rebuffed Iranian requests to return monies from the Shah's personal accounts which Tehran claimed were the property of the state and the Iranian people and had been stolen by the Shah for his personal gain and enrichment. The Iranians were also upset upon notification that the Shah was being permitted entry to the United States for medical treatment for his terminal pancreatic cancer diagnosis. Tehran demanded his extradition to stand trial for his crimes in Iran. When the United States proved unwilling or unable to persuade its allies in other countries where the Shah was seeking refuge to have him returned to Iran, university students embarked on a series of demonstrations at the US Embassy in Tehran. Upon storming the compound, they seized the premises and detained dozens of embassy officials, releasing most, but keeping captive 52 Americans until their eventual release in January 1981. The discovery of the CIA bureau office within the embassy, and the revelation of hundreds of communiques between the Shah and the CIA angered the protesters and the government, as they exposed the extent of coordination between the two entities in suppressing the Iranian people. The ensuing severance of diplomatic relations, and the asymmetric balance of power in the region led Iran's adversaries to exploit the country's international isolation by making it the centre of regional conflicts, and the target of decades of crippling sanctions and punitive measures. (Fisk, 2007)

The mercurial nature of American foreign policy toward Muslim states is a function of maintaining overall dominance over those countries and their strategic and commercial assets. Perceiving Iran post-Revolution as a threat to its regional strategic interests, due in large part to Iran's unwillingness to accept American hegemony over it any longer, the United States supported the dictatorship of Iraq's Saddam Hussein when he sought to exploit the relative instability of Iran after the Revolution. From 1980-1988, Iraq initiated and prosecuted a long and costly war against Iran. Hussein received the backing and support of Washington as well as several regional Arab states which also resented and feared an ascendant and explicit Persian, Shi'i regime. The war cost at least 1.5 million lives and ultimately failed to destabilize the Iranian government. (Fisk, 2007)

When Hussein's efforts against Iran proved to be unsuccessful, the Iraqi leader had exhausted his usefulness for Washington. His own ambition to acquire territory prompted him to invade Kuwait in August 1990, under the pretext that the emirate had been improperly denied to Iraq by the British in the aftermath of World War I. Because of his purported threat to Saudi Arabia, now America's main petroleum strategic ally in the region. The United States invaded Iraq in January 1991 to expunge Hussein's army from Kuwait and drive his forces back to Baghdad. After 9-11, under two false premises - Hussein's alleged complicity with Al Qaeda and Osama bin Laden to orchestrate the terrorist attacks and the allegation of Hussein possessing weapons of mass destruction - and over a decade of sanctions, embargoes and no-fly zones over the country, the United States invaded Iraq and ousted Saddam Hussein in 2003. Claims of removing a despot in favor of bringing democracy to Iraq and its people proved to be risible and hollow as it ran counter to a well-established record of American aversion to democratic regimes in the developing world that defied calls for sycophancy toward Washington. (Fisk, 2007)

The recent effort to bring some semblance of balance to American engagement in the Persian Gulf was the 2015 Joint Comprehensive Plan of Action (JCPOA), otherwise known as the Iran Nuclear Deal, an accord involving the five permanent members of the UN Security Council (US, Great Britain, France, Russia and China) as well as Germany, with Iran pledging to place a moratorium on the development of its military use nuclear weapons program. The Obama Administration that spearheaded the painstaking negotiations sought to leverage diplomatic processes to gain the confidence and trust of the Iranian regime to move toward a détente in its decades-old "cold war" with Saudi Arabia and other Gulf states such as the United Arab Emirates. Obama also recognized the need to develop a less antagonistic relationship with Tehran as a way for the US to repel the prospect of stronger ties between Iran and other world powers such as Russia and China. All such aims were dismantled when the Trump Administration unilaterally withdrew from the JCPOA in 2018, and President Donald Trump intensified the sanctions regimen against Iran, in a move designed to provoke a strong reaction from Tehran that could lead to a justification for American military action against the country. By no mere coincidence, the Trump Administration's closer ties to Saudi Arabia, the UAE, as well as the Netanyahu administration in Israel have all contributed to the shift in posture by the US government from one administration to the other. A key, and contrapuntal point of note is that despite the passage of the Iran nuclear deal and the expected, presumed de-escalation of potential military conflict in the region, the United States greatly increased its sale of weapons systems to several regional actors, including Saudi Arabia, the UAE, Israel and Qatar. It would appear that if the threat level had abated, so too would the need for additional conventional munitions. The incident demonstrates the cynical manufacture of crisis as an excuse for the United States to engage in lucrative defense contract transactions. (Fitzpatrick, 2019)

American foreign policy toward Saudi Arabia marks an 80 year-long commitment to the kingdom's security, more specifically, the protection and preservation of the House of Saud. Despite the fact that fifteen of the nineteen hijackers involved in the 9-11 terrorist attack were in fact Saudi nationals, no serious recriminations occurred for Riyadh. Similarly, and despite considerable global outrage at the murder of Saudi journalist and American resident Jamal Khashoggi in October 2018, at the hands of Saudi security agents in Istanbul, and, according to US intelligence sources, the knowledge if not purported authorization by Crown Prince Mohammed Bin Salman (MbS), US-Saudi relations suffered no damage. Instead, the Trump Administration offered a rare moment of lucid candor by declaring that Saudi commitments to purchase multi-billion dollar weapons systems were far more important and valuable to the US than the death of a journalist.

American influence in the Persian Gulf has moved beyond just Saudi Arabia. The United Arab Emirates has gradually ascended to a prominent, highly influential role in shaping American policy in the region over the past two decades. Similarly, Qatar and Bahrain have played instrumental roles in furnishing the American military presence with logistical and geostrategic assistance.

Cold War geopolitics put Muslim countries within the

maelstrom of US foreign policy assertions beyond the Middle East. Pakistan was founded in 1947, in the aftermath of a brutal struggle for independence from Great Britain and the concomitant partition from India. Within a dangerous neighborhood of two major communist powers - the Soviet Union and China, respectively- Pakistan played a perilous role as America's frontline ally in South Asia. For the United States, a stable ally in the region required political stability even at the expense of democracy. Pakistan's leadership has alternated between democracy, in some cases, corrupt, nepotistic ones, and martial law. Pakistan, as a member of CENTO, was obligated to furnish the United States with any and all necessary logistical resources in the war against the Soviet Bloc. A case in point is the 1960 U2 crisis involving US pilot Francis Gary Powers. The American Air Force officer took off from an air base in Pakistan to run reconnaissance sorties over the Soviet Union before he was shot down by a surface to air missile. While the matter was eventually resolved diplomatically between the two superpowers, front line countries like Pakistan invariably bore the vicarious brunt of Cold War policies. The Soviet Union gravitated more closely toward India, Pakistan's most consistent adversary in the region, supplying it with military and intelligence cooperation against Islamabad. (Nawaz, 2008)

Due to the inherently asymmetric nature of the relationship, Pakistan was often obliged to acquiesce to American requests, or more often demands, for cooperation. Pakistan served as the major conduit for supplies and weapons to the opposition forces in the decade-long Afghan war against the Soviet invasion of 1979. The collateral damage to Pakistan was the influx of millions of Afghan refugees and the introduction of Islamic fundamentalism, the opium industry and gun lawlessness throughout the country; the legacy of destabilization it brought still plagues the country today. Similarly, Pakistan was forced to resume its role as American satrap during the post-9-11 invasion of Afghanistan to fight Al Qaeda and the Taliban. American officials openly acknowledge that they issued then Pakistani leader Parvez Musharraf an ultimatum that Pakistani refusal to cooperate would make the country the next target in American crosshairs after Afghanistan.

American policy toward Muslim states in the 21st century has continued to be mercurial at best and devised more for transactional than transcendental reasons. The United States was willing to allow a thirty year relationship with Egyptian dictator Hosni Mubarak yield to the popular will of reform in 2011. Washington was similarly silent when Mubarak's successor, the democratically elected Mohammad Morsi, was deposed two years later in a counter coup.

American ignorance about Middle East geopolitics beyond petroleum has caused it to defer much of its understanding of the region to local actors who bring their own strong biases, agendas and priorities to the fold. In 1958, convinced by Israel, former colonial actors like Great Britain and France, as well as petro-states like Saudi Arabia, of the purported danger of Egyptian leader Gamal Abdel Nasser, Washington responded in 1958 to a plea by President Camille Chamoun to deploy US marines to Lebanon to quell popular unrest and protests against his ineffective government. Thus started a decades long record of American intervention and encroachment into a region US policy makers do not fully understand. Goaded into believing that perceived threats to local entities were also grave threats to American national security, the United States has played both direct and indirect roles in adding to the regional instability. (Sayigh, 2003)

US Marines returned to Lebanon in 1983, in the midst of the country's toxic civil war. Ostensibly, their presence was listed as a peacekeeping mission, though it was a means by which to police the Palestine Liberation Organization, which was operating from Lebanon after Israel invaded the country in 1982. The Marines' presence was opposed as a gross encroachment and unnecessary addition to the ongoing conflict. In October 1983, suicide bombers stormed the Marine enclave, detonating explosive-laden vehicles. 241 Marines' died as a result. While the United States blamed Iran, Hezbollah and a host of Muslim related entities, lost in the calculus of accountability was the actual causation for their presence- the uninvited interference in a civil war, ostensibly to protect Israel after its incursion the year before, as well as retribution for the brutal massacre of an estimated 3,500 civilians in the Sabra-Shatilla refugee camps, by Christian Phalange forces, aided by Israeli military elements. Of course, notwithstanding such direct American involvement in crises in the Middle East and the Muslim world writ large, US involvement is also pronounced and impactful by way of the weapons it sells local and regional actors and the manner in which they are deployed against Muslims. A large percentage of the Israeli Defense Forces arsenal is American made, and has been repeatedly used in various campaigns in the Palestinian Territories, including during the First (1987-1993) and Second (2000-2005) Intifadas, as well as more recent campaigns including Operation Cast Lead (2008) and Operation Protective Edge (2014) in Gaza. (Tal, 2019)

State Relations with Muslims since 9-11

The relationship of the state with the American Muslim community since 9-11 has been one primarily shaped through the lens of securitization. Of course, government efforts at targeting suspect demographic groups is nothing new in the United States. The so-called COINTEL programs of the FBI have been used to surveil communities based on racial, ethnic and ideological classifications. Throughout the 1950s and 60s, the African-American community and especially the civil rights movement faced the glaring scrutiny of FBI director J. Edgar Hoover and his suspicions that black America was an existential threat to the nation. As with the case of the communist hysteria, the so-called red scare in the 1950s, any group deemed to be subversive even without evidence to affirm such a charge, would endure investigation, interrogation and policies which clearly represented a breach of privacy and a breach of civil liberties. (Curtis, 2013)

In 1914, Marcus Garvey, a Jamaican-American political activist and founder of the United Negro Improvement Association and African Communities League, established The Negro World, a gazette that addressed the needs of the African-American community. Garvey advocated for African Americans to gain financial independence from the white majority and promoted black empowerment. Garvey also touted the importance of pan-Africanism, a movement that united all people of color especially on the African continent. Given the long and rich history of Islam in Africa, Garvey expounded upon the natural and organic link between Pan-Africanism and Islam.

Garvey's eloquence and influence did not go unnoticed by American authorities, who saw him as a threat to the white establishment within the United States and more broadly, as a threat to the European colonial enterprise globally. Garvey became the target of a sustained campaign of surveillance and harassment by government authorities, who feared his ability to embolden minority communities to defy institutional racism, discrimination and the status quo of the white establishment. Garvey's perspectives and activism were highly influential within the African American Muslim community, particularly with the Nation of Islam and Malcolm X, for whom Garvey's black nationalism was a key ideological foundation. (GhaneaBissari, 2010)

For Muslim Americans, surveillance has been a two-pronged historical phenomenon. The Nation of Islam faced such scrutiny during the 1960s with the classical example being of civil rights leader Malcolm X. In that case, the Nation of Islam and government action against it was part of the broader surveillance of the African-American community; after all, even other leaders of the black community like Dr. Martin Luther King Jr. and the Black Panthers, including Huey Newton and Bobby Seale, were subjected to the broader panopticon of surveillance. For immigrant Muslims, the realization that they too were the object of investigation came to prominence after the 1993 World Trade Center bombing. (GhaneaBissari, 2010)

The USA Patriot Act was enacted by the US Congress and signed into law by President George W. Bush on October 26, 2001 a mere five weeks after the 9-11 attacks. (United States, 2001) The procurement of this legislation is a testament to the hysteria that gripped both the country and in particular the government in the days and weeks after the terrorist attacks. Many politicians who voted for the USA Patriot Act conceded that they had barely read any of its 342 pages before casting their fateful and decisive votes to pass it. Before it reached the President's desk, the bill passed the Congress by a 357-66 margin and the Senate by an overwhelming 98-1 vote. It is quite clear that most legislators did not wish to appear weak or uncommitted to the full effort of combating terrorism in the aftermath of 9-11. (Etzioni, 2005) As such, otherwise thoughtful deliberation and debate upon the constitutionality of the act, as well as the consequences on the civil liberties and privacy rights of American citizens, were completely ignored in the zeal to demonstrate to the American public that elected officials were providing the President and the executive branch with any and all tactics and tools they would require to prevent any additional attacks on US soil. One may reasonably infer that political hysteria and the due deference given by the American public for such efforts in the name of safety and security were done so based on the presumption that the only targets of such sweeping and intrusive legislation would be those most deserving and suspected of malfeasance, i.e. Muslim Americans. It did not occur to the vast majority of the American public what would be the ramifications of such legislation going beyond the Muslim community and its application. In effect, the majority of the American public felt itself immune from scrutiny, surveillance and encroachment, all of which would be inevitable results of this legislation. Even the official title given to this legislation (Uniting and Strengthening America by Providing Appropriate Tools Required to Intercept and Obstruct Terrorism (USA PATRIOT) Act of 2001) made clear the implications for civil liberties. The rather less bulky acronym USA Patriot Act was intended to invoke a high-level of jingoism and challenge any dissenters who might question its scope, scale and extent of encroachment, not to mention its constitutionality, to have to prove their allegiance to the country.

The American government claimed that the USA Patriot Act would provide invaluable assistance for it to combat terrorism in myriad ways. Among these would be efforts to combat money laundering which could be used to finance terrorism. In addition, the Act would allow government agencies the ability to engage in enhanced surveillance of suspects, be they individuals or organizations. Conventional constitutional safeguards such as due process, especially for US citizens, were now considered immaterial in the greater professed objective of national security. As a result, and with the effective use of the FISA courts, an untold number of Muslim Americans were subjected to enhance surveillance which included access to voicemail messages, text messages and emails. Much of these encroachments were facilitated by the cooperation of telecommunications and internet companies. Section 215 of the USA Patriot Act in fact allowed the

US government to obtain secret court orders requiring telephone and other communications companies to hand over anything that the government regarded to be relevant to an ongoing international investigation of counterespionage, foreign intelligence or terrorism. (Love, 2017)

Another area of encroachment facilitated by the USA Patriot Act was border security. Given the fact that the 9-11 hijackers had made their way legally into the United States, the US government was concerned weather so-called sleeper cells or other individuals were making their way into the country for further terrorist acts. Government officials were also scrutinizing travel patterns, especially of Muslim Americans and more specifically if they were to and from Muslim countries. In some cases, Muslims were placed on no-fly lists, without any explanation and with few if any avenues of recourse to have their names removed. In addition, many Muslim Americans experienced various elements of racial and religious profiling, the so-called "flying while Muslim" phenomenon. (Love, 2017) This could entail additional security measures, including the risible "randomly selected for additional screening" measures, or being subjected to having one's baggage searched by security officials. If such additional screening resulted in missing one's flight, the passenger had no recourse to compensation. At best, he or she could request the airline to place him or her on a subsequent flight, subject to availability. Not all of the profiling of Muslim American passengers was conducted by government or security officials; the climate of the post 9-11, USA Patriot Act era effectively deputized civil society to do its best to be vigilant in the so-called war on terror. If a fellow passenger felt uncomfortable seeing a Muslim on board the flight, he or she could alert a member of the flight crew to have the Muslim passenger removed. Similarly, the captain, who has categorical authority on board the aircraft, would be fully within his or her discretion to remove a Muslim passenger without much cause. Irrespective of a lack of probable cause or even good faith, the affected Muslim passenger would have no recourse against the airline, the captain or the accuser; all could escape accountability with complete impunity. (Love, 2017)

Muslim passenger profiling was a function of an algorithm and set of criteria that the US government was unwilling to divulge to the public in the name of national security. While government officials claimed that they were not specifically targeting individuals based on race or religion, it was glaringly obvious that Muslims faced a disproportionate level of scrutiny within the government's pursuits. The profiled individual's age, name, place of birth, ethnicity, national origin, gender and even marital status all provided a sketch of a certain kind of suspect for security agencies. Particularly suspect to profiling were Muslim single males between the ages of 18 and 50. At the same time, however, even Muslim children as young as two years of age found their names on no-fly lists and/or scrutiny at airports. For US authorities, the Muslim name was the true incriminating factor, irrespective of the fact that the so-called suspect was still wearing diapers. (Love, 2017)

Some Muslim passengers re-entering the United States, either by land from Canada or Mexico, or by air, were subjected to hours of questioning upon arrival. These interrogations were conducted without the passenger having the benefit of counsel to assist him or her. In some instances, Muslim passengers were escorted off their flights by security officials, with no explanation given, before the rest of the passengers were allowed to disembark,

Under the USA Patriot Act, even mosques and Islamic schools faced enhanced scrutiny and surveillance by the US government. Security officials placed these facilities under a host of investigative tactics, including the use of wiretaps to surveil mosque officials and imams, install listening devices to hear sermons and even send informants to spy on conversations of mosque attendees. Some of these undercover agents posed as converts to Islam, in some cases, acting in an intentionally and overly zealous manner, making provocative, extremist statements as a way to entrap the innocent. In other situations, the federal agencies would employ native informants who were promised expungement of their criminal records or the opportunity to satisfy a personal vendetta against a fellow congregant. (Love, 2017) The overall impact of such tactics was to create a cloud of suspicion within the Muslim American community whereby any unfamiliar face was now viewed with suspicion that he or she could be a government operative. It did not take long for the sense of being a securitized community to become internalized by Muslim Americans throughout the country.

In addition to the USA Patriot Act, the US government vigorously made use of the Foreign Intelligence Surveillance Act of 1978 which established the so-called FISA courts whereby the government may seek warrants for searches, arrests or wire taps where it suspects an individual or a group of spying for a foreign entity or for belonging to a terrorist organization. Since their inception, the FISA courts have issued hundreds of warrants annually. Their rejection rate is extremely low; in fact, over several years, notwithstanding hundreds of FISA requests, the courts have a 100% acceptance rate. Part of the controversy surrounding the FISA courts is that they operate in near complete secrecy. In addition, there is little to no ability for a targeted individual or group to either be aware that they are under surveillance or have any recourse to appeal the action taken against them. The government enjoys near absolute deference by FISA court judges, who are loathe to rebut the presumption of necessity and even good faith by government officials requesting such warrants. (Love, 2017)

Since 9-11, FISA court requests have nearly all involved Muslim suspects either as individuals, organizations or even institutions. These have involved mosques, Islamic schools and Muslim charities. (Love, 2017) While the stated goal of FISA court requests for warrants has been to survey all suspected foreign spies or members in terrorist groups, it seems as though the dragnet has been far broader than the FISA laws mandate allows. Investigative research now shows that several prominent Muslim Americans have been targeted by highly intrusive surveillance programs. Among them are Faisal Gill, who was a prominent Muslim within the Republican Party. He was also at the Department of Homeland Security, with top-secret clearance, under the administration of President George W Bush. Another prominent Muslim American subjected to face such action was Asim Ghafoor, a lawyer representing individuals charged with terrorism. Academics were also not spared from FISA record requests. Agha Saeed, a former political science professor at California State University and outspoken advocate for Muslim civil liberties and Palestinian rights, and Hooshang Amiraahmadi, professor of international relations at Rutgers University, were both surveilled by the US government. But perhaps the most high-profile target of a FISA court warrant was Nihad Awad, the executive Director of the

Council on American Islamic Relations, the largest Muslim American civil rights organization. (Greenwald, 2014)

Today, debates about the propriety of the FISA courts have finally gone mainstream in the American public discourse. Recently, government officials have used FISA court requests to surveil all individuals with connections to the Trump administration. It is no coincidence that some of the strongest voices of outrage at both the secrecy and scope of the FISA warrants and the system under which they are obtained happened to be among the strongest supporters of President Trump and his administration. These same individuals, whether in the US Congress or in the US Senate, rabidly advocated for the critical need for the FISA court system when the intended targets were almost exclusively Muslim Americans. Now that the scope of scrutiny has proven to extend beyond just one, seemingly acceptable suspect group, the moral outrage has reached fever pitch in public debate. The legitimacy of a government program, validating acceptable bigotry against a single, "foreign" group, whose American-ness has apparently always been viewed circumspectly, has given way to a rare moment of reflection when it has been demonstrated that the laws may in fact be applied to other Americans as well. In so doing, the FISA court controversy yet again affirms that for the erosion of American civil liberties and a reasonable expectation of privacy, Muslim Americans were used as proverbial guinea pigs to experiment with acceptable public intrusions into the privacy of American citizens. Muslim Americans therefore became canaries in the coal mine, whereby the government could test both constitutional and civic boundaries.

The state relationship with Muslim Americans also includes efforts to ban Muslims from entering the United States. During his candidacy, Donald Trump announced that he supported a full and total ban on Muslims entering the country. He claimed that his declaration was due to his perceived confusion at how immigration policy was being implemented by the government. True to his word, President Trump issued an executive order one week after taking the oath of office which banned entry to the United States for citizens from Muslim countries such as Syria, Yemen, Iraq, Iran, Sudan, Libya and Somalia. After strenuous opposition and litigation efforts, the president modified his executive order to include non-Muslim countries like Venezuela and North Korea. (Love, 2017) Nonetheless, both Trump's actions and clearly stated intent on several occasions made clear that the president was targeting Muslims. Trump became emboldened by the Supreme Court's decision authorizing his right to regulate immigration based on his position as head of the executive branch of government. To date, these bans are still in effect, despite the initial statement that they would be temporary for some of the affected countries. The overall effect on Muslim Americans has been one of disruption as it severely jeopardizes and prevents families from seeking unification, a key and long-held American objective of immigration policies.

Not all state relations with Muslim Americans has occurred at the federal/national level. In fact, there have been several actions taken at the state level which have stigmatized and targeted the Muslim community. The most notorious of such efforts has taken place across the country in as many as 38 of the 50 state legislatures, where politicians have sponsored or co-sponsored legislation seeking to ban the consideration and application of Islamic law in judicial proceedings. The so-called anti-sharia bills have been struck down by the courts as being blatantly unconstitutional due to their vagueness and over scope. The courts have cited the first amendment of the U.S. Constitution and its guarantees for the free exercise of religion as being a paramount defense against such highly political and politicized legislative efforts. Within the United States, there is a long-held acceptance of consideration for religious-based laws in various judicial proceedings, particularly in matters of family law. For example, the state of New York will recognize a Jewish divorce, *get*, that has been procured by rabbinical authorities. Similarly, Muslim Americans commonly seek to enforce from American courts matters of divorce, inheritance, custody and various other legal issues in compliance with Islamic sensibilities. Muslim Americans have not sued to have sharia codified as a parallel or superior legal system that would eclipse or subvert the US Constitution or other laws, either at the federal or state levels. They have merely attempted to gain similar recognition for their particular religious matters as have various religious communities before them including both Catholics and Jews. This has been perhaps most visible when it comes to holidays and dietary considerations;

Catholics have sought recognition for meatless Fridays as have Jews for the availability of kosher food, both in public schools and places of employment where the holiday calendar and menus tend to presume compliance with the majority Protestant American ethos.

Nonetheless, zealous politicians have striven to create the "Phantom Menace" of sharia law and the specter of fear that non-Muslims would somehow be subjected and subjugated by an oppressive expression of Islamic law. Such legislative efforts gained their highest level of success, actual passage of the bills into law, in states which have conservative or Republican majority in the state legislature. The first such action occurred in Oklahoma in 2010. (Oklahoma, 2010) The Muslim community in that state is very small in population and certainly does not pose a threat to broader society. However, its relatively minimal social and political capital made it an easy target for those seeking to score political points among a bigoted constituency that was as ignorant of the US Constitution as it was about Islam itself. While none of the attempted anti-sharia bills has successfully been enacted into law, the impact on the Muslim American community has been undeniable. It has stigmatized the community by showing the contempt and bigotry of those individuals who purport to be the elected representatives for all state citizens, Muslim or otherwise. In addition, efforts to combat such legislation is quite costly, and is an unnecessary drain on already limited community resources. But perhaps the most long lasting impact of such conflicts is the internalization of being perceived as an acceptable target and an alien, pernicious presence whereby a Muslim American's allegiance to the country and society is always open to scrutiny and where the Muslim always has to refute the presumption that he or she is disloyal, a risk or threat.

Efforts to implement anti-sharia laws in the United States complemented similar efforts to ban mosque construction or expansion. One of the most prominent cases in this regard involved the Islamic Center of Murfreesboro, a community outside Nashville, Tennessee, and home to Middle Tennessee State University, an institution that was home to international students, including several from Muslim countries. In 2010, the Murfreesboro Muslim community sought to construct a mosque and an adjacent cemetery on land that it had purchased. The community went through the normal channels of seeking approval from the local planning commission. However, a tremendous backlash was led by several opponents to such a project, both local and even nationally. The ensuing litigation exposed a tremendous amount of bigotry, from politicians, religious and community leaders, as well as propelling the story into a national issue, whereby Islamophobes framed the incident as an example of Muslim encroachment into the so-called Bible Belt of America. One of the attorneys representing the opponents to the mosque construction even questioned whether Islam was an actual religion. The audacity of his claim was rebutted by no less than the attorney general of the United States, Eric Holder, who issued a declaration on behalf of the Obama administration that Islam is in fact a well-established, globally recognized, legitimate religion. (Kar, 2010) The issue with the attorney's outlandish conduct was not that he had any reasonable prospects for making a successful argument; it was his more sinister effort to cast doubt on the legitimacy of Islam and thereby seek to extricate Islam, and Muslims as a group, from the constitutional protections afforded recognized religions to free exercise of those faiths, by the First Amendment. Fortunately, the rule of law prevailed, and the Islamic center of Murfreesboro was granted its request to construct its mosque. The victory was hard fought and not without considerable challenges. The construction site was vandalized and the target of arson. In the early stages of the controversy, both mosque officials as well as Muslim congregants were subjected to a fusillade of profanity, acerbic comments and demonization by the local community. At the same time, however, there were many members of Murfreesboro's faith community and social justice activists who embraced the issue to provide much-needed solidarity and support for the city's Muslim community.

Chapter 2

Muslim Expectations and Concerns

"American Issues"

Political engagement is a fundamental feature of American civic life. Candidacy for, and election to, public office is considered the pinnacle of the process of being "American." The impetus for greater Muslim representation in the political arena certainly gained greater momentum after the 9-11 attacks as did the American Muslim community's recognition that having Muslims in office could best and most accurately meet its needs. Given the toxic climate around Muslim identity due to the 2001 attacks, the various US military campaigns in the Middle East and South Asia and the ensuing reactions to them, Islam became perceived as a foreign, menacing, threatening presence within the United States. It is quite telling that the first Muslims elected to prominent and visible office were African American Muslims. Given the complex and sordid history of American racial politics, the religious affiliation of the politicians was subsumed to their racial identity. Bigoted attacks on their race would not be accepted readily in the public debates, and as a result, the expected aspersions against their religion were relatively muted. It is also important to consider that virtually all Muslim Americans elected to public office are from the Democratic Party, which both embraced the inclusion of Muslims in a far more open manner than the Republican Party, which not only offered a frosty reception to Muslims but openly trafficked in divisive and acerbic rhetoric against Islam and Muslims as a political tool.

The first elected Muslim to the United States Congress was Keith Ellison from Minnesota in 2006. He very famously took his oath of office holding the Qur'an of American founding father and third President Thomas Jefferson. Of course, he was met with his fair share of detractors, who accused Ellison of being a stealth Islamist who planned to implement sharia law once seated in Congress. Conservative critics also contended that Ellison's oath was invalid as the Qur'an was not the Bible and thus void and meaningless declaration. (Rosenberg, 2019) Either unknown to his critics or aware but unconcerned about their disparagements based on falsehoods, the oath of office that involves a book of scripture is merely symbolic, irrespective of whether a Bible, Torah, Qur'an or Bhagavad Gita is used. The actual, and formal, oath of office occurs with the entire congressional delegation and involves the Representatives simply raising their right hands and swearing to support and defend the United States' Constitution against all enemies, foreign and domestic. Still, the optics of a Muslim congressman using a book other than the Bible provided ammunition to bigots and political opponents alike. Ellison served six two-year terms before deciding to seek state level office. In 2018, Ellison was elected Minnesota's Attorney General, the highest-ranking law enforcement office in the state, and, of course, the first Muslim to gain the office.

Like Keith Ellison, Andre Carson is an African American Muslim, entering the United States Congress from the State of Indiana in 2008, replacing his deceased mother in her congressional seat. He ran for office and was elected in his own right in late 2008, and has successfully won reelection ever since. He is a member of the important and powerful House Select Committee on Intelligence, which has played a prominent role in investigating allegations of corruption and illegal activity by the Trump administration.

2018 became a watershed year for Muslim American candidates and electoral victories. Ironically, the 2016 election of Donald Trump served as the greatest catalyst to embolden and empower Muslims to seek political office. His toxic rhetoric during his candidacy, especially with his declaration that, "Islam hates us," and his ensuing, improbable election victory, served as a clarion call for Muslims to mobilize both at the ballot box as well as placing their names on the ballots themselves. According to the Muslim American political engagement organization, Emgage, over 100 Muslims ran for office in various local, state and national races, and over 55 won their respective elections. Currently, over 300 Muslims nationwide hold political office.

Building on the national visibility and prominence of Keith Ellison and Andre Carson, immigrant Muslim Americans entered the fray with high profile candidacies. Rashida Tlaib, a Palestinian-American lawyer and former state representative from Michigan, won her congressional seat in 2018, becoming one of the first two Muslim American women elected to the

United States Congress. She was joined by Ilhan Omar, a Muslim from Minnesota who came to the United States as a refugee, fleeing the turmoil in her native Somalia in 1992. After serving in the Minnesota State House, Omar successfully won election to Congress from Keith Ellison's former congressional district. Omar's compelling personal story fit into the pervasive American narrative of the country being a welcoming land of opportunity for people escaping turmoil and tyranny overseas. Of course, that narrative is openly challenged and refuted by the Trump administration and the President's supporters, who crave a more xenophobic and exclusivist policy toward immigration, both legal and otherwise, including the imposition of strict and severe curbs on the entry of refugees. (Gajanan, 2018)

The election of Rashida Tlaib and Ilhan Omar has proved to be a source of tremendous inspiration for Muslim Americans, especially for young Muslim women, who see tenacious and committed role models that are change agents at the highest level, especially Omar, whose headscarf denotes a visible and explicit connection to Islam. At the same time, however, both Tlaib and Omar have been consistent targets for Islamophobes misogynists and conservatives who detest positive examples of Muslim Americans in the public sphere. Both congresswomen self-identify as progressives, aligned with the left side of the Democratic Party's ideological spectrum. They have both been very vocal not only with issues they champion but have also been harsh critics of President Trump, his policies and his alleged corrupt conduct. Trump himself has routinely taken to Twitter and other social media platforms to excoriate both Tlaib and Omar, impugning them for their politics, gender, religious affiliation and their ethnicity. He has openly challenged their loyalty to the United States and even suggested they should leave the country if they are so critical of his policies. The President's supporters have heeded his example and intensified the criticisms, including the issuance of death threats against both Tlaib and Omar.

The visibility and accomplishments of Muslim American politicians has a domino effect for the community. As they become more aware of both political issues and the logistics of the political process and the viability of electoral success, more Muslim Americans, especially younger Muslims, are considering a career in politics. Beyond running for political office at the local, state and national offices, Muslim Americans are entering the political arena as interns and staff members for politicians, gaining invaluable experience and insight into the machinations of America's complex political process. The campaign manager for Senator Bernie Sanders and his bid for President in the 2020 elections is Faiz Shakir, a Muslim American with considerable experience in government at a variety of federal agencies and posts and as a policy advisor.

Similarly, Muslim Americans are understanding the importance of policy making as a vital complement of the political arena. As a result, many are increasing their profile and input with think tanks and policy centers that examine social, domestic policy issues as well as providing contributions to foreign policy matters. The diffusion of Muslim Americans into the political channels is a critical step toward Muslims gaining an essential voice and representation beyond just elected office.

The Muslim population in the United States is estimated to be somewhere between 3.5-8 million, depending upon the survey that is consulted. As such, it constitutes approximately 1-2.5% of the total American population. (Pew Research Center, 2017) While many are located in concentrated communities in several metropolitan areas, their political and social capital remains fairly diluted, leading to the ease by which the community is harangued and at times demonized. The community is also, arguably, the most diverse Muslim population in the world, comprising of people representing every conceivable race, ethnicity, denomination, ideology and socio-economic level. It is a community that is constantly growing, as a result of three major causes. First, immigration, even with recent restrictions from so-called Muslim countries, allows for a consistent, fluid influx of Muslim immigrants. Second, there is the natural growth of the community through marriage and reproduction. Lastly, conversion to Islam has increased the population; the Latin American Muslim community, for example, is the fasting growing contingent in the country.

While there is no theological obligation for uniformity, unity within the American Muslim community remains an elusive issue. The various tectonic plates within the community risk the prospect of manifesting themselves as ambivalence and dismissiveness to outright antipathy toward a specific subgroup. There are various affiliations based on ideological lines, ranging from fundamentalist to moderately, mildly observant or non-observant; "conservative," "moderate" and "liberal" or "progressive." These lines of demarcation gain added complexity when conflating political and theological considerations in an ever changing American social landscape. They are often a combination of proactive formulations of identity construction, both normative and empirical, as well as reaction and adaptation to evolving processes in society, both within the Muslim American community as well as the country writ large.

Sectarian difference is nothing new in Islamic societies and such diversity is clearly evident within the United States. In many ways, the denominational demographics in America reflect the global reality, with Sunni Muslims comprising the vast majority of the population, although certain areas of the country may have larger Shi'i communities, e.g. Dearborn, Michigan. Liturgical differences usually evolve into the development of parallel institutions, i.e. mosques that are considered "Shi'i" or "Sunni," with sometimes further distinctions based on the ideological inclination of the facility. While never explicitly stated, most Muslims have an understanding of the composition and affiliation of the respective mosques in their locale and use that information to decide where to attend, both for prayer and other religious observance as well as for social engagement. Some mosques are known by the majority ethnic group that are its members. There are "Arab" mosques and "South Asian" mosques and more recently, even more particularized facilities, such as "Bangladeshi" vs "Indian/Pakistani" mosques. Such distinctions are often a function of the *lingua franca* within the mosque, both theologically as well as socially. The decision to affiliate with a particular mosque is often invoked by immigrant Muslims as a way to stay connected to language and culture of the countries of national origin, as well as a method to make children acquainted to the "home" country and its traditions. At the same time, another inevitable consequence is the Balkanization of the community into arbitrary and artificial silos. The danger is that subsequent generations of Muslim Americans face estrangement from one another due to these barriers to a formative arena of their socialization. The implications can then affect not only interaction as children, but stifle the potential for cross-cultural marriage and the perception that culture supersedes religion as the primary identity marker for Muslim Americans.

Socio-economic divisions play as significant a role in dividing the Muslim American community as ideological and sectarian factors. Mosques and other Islamic institutions in suburban locales tend to serve affluent Muslim populations compared to their inner-city counterparts. This creates dramatic differences as to the resources each center possesses and can offer its membership. Oftentimes, such socio-economic distinctions are accompanied by racial or ethnic difference; in many large American cities, the African American Muslim community is concentrated in urban settings that have limited resources for their mosques, schools and other facilities. The level of inter-communal engagement is a serious challenge, as the chasm between the affluent suburbs and modest inner city communities manifests itself in limited, if any, meaningful interaction. Undergirding the community gap is the added specter of intrafaith racism.

The reality and importance of socio-economics have played an incalculable role in the development of Islam in the United States. For Muslim immigrants, there was a sense of urgency to establish institutions that meet community needs. Moreover, due to limited resources coupled with multiple requirements, the priority was to create multipurpose institutions. In their so-called "home" countries, the religious institutions, i.e. mosques, are just religious spaces. Social engagement has the entire communal landscape in which to operate. In the United States, Muslim immigrants saw the mosque as being the one-stop religious and social haven, particularly with a dominant cultural paradigm that was sufficiently different and permissive in ways that would run afoul of Islamic tenets. As these mosques were established, they tended to have a dominant cultural and/or ethnic identity attributed to them it as a function of their key founders. As in other non-Muslim majority countries, Islamic centers in the United States are often identified as "Arab" or "Indo-Pak" mosques. Much of the social programming, as well as the theological instruction beyond the prayers and part of the sermons (*khutbas*) are conducted in the dominant immigrant language of the center. This reflects the status of the mosque as the location for religious and social edification, and the desire for attendees to attempt to preserve both cultural and religious ties. Of course, the privileging of one language, other than a unifying language like English, will by definition exclude others who are unfamiliar with that language. Unsurprisingly, it becomes a significant barrier between immigrant and African American Muslim communities.

The American Muslim community has a diverse and well sustained history that can be documented as an identifiable entity for at least a century in the United States. While the majority of Muslims immigrated over the past 60 years, the fact that they were arriving into a new, strange land with at least some coreligionist presence would have been cause for much relief and sense of comfort. Unfortunately, the organic and harmonious comingling of the existing Muslim community and the more recent arrivals has been far from a smooth process; in fact, it has been at times quite tense.

As Muslims began to arrive in large numbers from across the so-called Muslim world in the mid-1960s onwards, they encountered an existing Muslim community that bore little ideological resemblance, let alone cultural familiarity. Much of this dissonance was the product of skepticism about the authenticity of the Islam practised by African American Muslims, especially those belonging to the Nation of Islam. Given the heavy emphasis on racial identity as well as the political impetus of the Nation's black nationalism, immigrant Muslims felt estranged from the ability to achieve a common "language" of engagement. As immigrant Muslims established various institutions and organizations in the United States, there was a reticence to bring African American Muslims into these community investments due to the perceived and professed differences of experience, ideology and sets of priorities.

1979 proved to be a pivotal year in the Muslim world. Several significant events occurred which forever shifted both the Muslim perception about Islam as well as the world's perception about Muslims. The year began with the Iranian Revolution and the ouster of the last Shah of Iran, Mohammad Reza Pahlavi, and the return from exile to Tehran of Ayatollah Khomeini, who led the nation and its people into a new era and a new future. 1979 was also the year of the Soviet invasion of Afghanistan and the emergence of a new and acceptable Muslim group, as it was seen to be doing the West's bidding: the Mujahideen, or Afghan freedom fighter. The Grand Mosque of Mecca, Islam's holiest site, was invaded and hundreds of pilgrims held hostage by a group of fanatic Saudi extremists who were upset by what they perceived to be the decadence and hypocrisy of the Saudi royal family. Turmoil in Lebanon with that country's civil war, the backlash within and against Egypt for signing the Camp David Peace Accords with Israel and the return of martial law at the hands of an Islamist dictator in Pakistan were other noteworthy episodes of a rather tumultuous year. The Muslim community in the United States, while thousands of miles away, was not immune to the changes occurring at break-neck speed throughout the ummah. The community had to cope with the critical shift in public perception that now redefined Islam.

Prior to 1979, the "public face" of Islam, i.e. how non-Muslims living in the United States perceived it, was generally defined and represented by the African American Muslim community. The most recognizable Muslims would be the late Malcolm X, Muhammad Ali and basketball great Kareem Abdul Jabbar. By 1979, although he was past his athletic prime, Ali had attained the stature of being a beloved American hero, a cultural icon and a global ambassador for the United States as well as for Islam. Similarly, Kareem Abdul-Jabbar, formerly Lew Alcindor, was a superstar center for the Los Angeles Lakers, one of the most dominant players in the history of the sport. But the Iranian Revolution took on an inadvertent American angle that changed how the nation engaged with Islam. The storming of the US Embassy in Tehran and the eventual captivity of 52 American embassy workers as hostages for 444 days became etched in the public imagination of Muslims, a legacy that persists to this day. It was from that moment that an American public that was generally ambivalent toward Islam became hostile. It was also the moment when the American notion of Islam transformed from a domestic, relatively benign, even somewhat positive force to one that was foreign, menacing and threatening. For many Americans, especially those who were exposed to a nearly nightly update on the hostage crisis, the new face of Islam was not

Muhammad Ali; it was Ayatollah Khomeini. The ramifications of this paradigm shift has affected everything from American Muslim identity construction and consciousness to how Black American and Immigrant Muslim relations occur and develop.

The Muslim American community, with its tremendous diversity across several lines of demarcation, is in effect a microcosm of broader American society. Unsurprisingly, the community shares similar concerns about the direction of the nation and its future. In national surveys, such as those conducted by the Pew Research Center, Muslims are concerned with and prioritize issues at a rate consistent with other religious groups in the country (Pew Research Center, 2007). Among the chief areas of focus are the quality of education for their children, both at the primary/secondary level as well as within higher education. In addition, the growing financial burdens associated with a university education affect Muslim and non-Muslim households alike. Muslim Americans are also concerned with the employment landscape for themselves and their children. With the volatility of global and national economies, Muslims are also contending with the rising influence of artificial intelligence and automation and the risks they bring to every sector of career and profession.

Health care and access to affordable and quality medical services is another key area of concern for Muslim Americans and a topic that places them well within the mainstream of awareness of American social issues. As the United States is the only major industrialized nation without universal health care, the issue of affordable healthcare has been a matter of policy as well as a highly politicized imperative, especially during election campaigns. Muslim Americans are well represented in the health sciences, as physicians, pharmacists and physical therapists, and offer insight on the complexities inherent within the healthcare debates.

The Muslim community of America is arguably the most diverse expression in the world and one of the most diverse demographic groups in the United States. An amalgam of every race, sect, ethnicity and linguistic family, no single subcategory can lay claim to being the quintessential Muslim American. But cultural racism allows the labeler to transcend otherwise unacceptable markers of bigotry, i.e. color vis-à-vis African

American Muslims, and focus on matters of culture as refracted through liturgy or religious obligation being inimical to the "sensitivities" of majority society. While the rhetoric levelled against Muslims may appear to be couched in terms of ideology or theology- in the case of Islam, the hackneyed accusation that its imperious nature will oblige its adherents to conquer America through the spread of its law and tenets- the impetus is a familiar xenophobia based on both nativism and Orientalism. While the public debate becomes obfuscated with alarmist concerns for "sharia law," "stealth jihadists" and an existential threat to "American values," the underlying antipathy appears less a function of Muslims for *what* they are; instead, it is based on the fact *that* they are.

This resulting racism is at once color-blind and yet also similar to the forms of racism that are color-based in that nuance and subtle difference are immaterial to the labeler; the only requirement to be a target is the identification as a Muslim. The individual's level of self-identification, assimilation into dominant society or even depth of piety becomes meaningless. Such bigotry may thus more accurately be defined as Muslimophobia than Islamophobia.

Given the sordid racial history of the United States and the demonization of various religious and ethnic suspect groups, one may rightly ask why the country, or at least some segments of it, has failed to learn from its past and assumed a more conciliatory, even welcoming, posture toward those that don't seem to fit a certain paradigm. A common rejoinder is to mention the terrorist attacks of September 11, 2001 and the fact that Muslims were the perpetrators. Furthermore, one could argue that the toll of two wars in Muslim countries- Iraq and Afghanistan- as well as the Ft. Hood shootings by Major Nidal Malik Hassan and the attempted bombing of Times Square in New York by Faisal Shehzad could affect attitudes toward Muslims. While a plausible cause for the intensified backlash against Muslim Americans, these events do not explain statistics regarding public opinion about Islam and Muslims. Immediately after the 9-11 attacks, American attitudes toward Muslims were less negative than they are today. This appears to be counterintuitive; the passage of time since 9-11 would, arguably, reduce the emotional trauma associated with that event and allow people to resist the temptation to impute collective guilt upon a people. Yet, this has not happened. The level of acrimony toward Muslims and Islam has attained a new intensity and even the ambivalent have decided to take a side in the debate. A decade after the worst attack on American soil, why are perceptions of Muslims deteriorating even further? Perhaps the answers lie beyond examining the trope of Islamophobia as a disease in itself. Instead, perhaps it may be beneficial to locate attitudes toward Muslims as a symptom of a broader, deeper social disease affecting the American psyche that is part of this nation's ongoing culture wars.

The phenomenon of anti-Muslim sentiment that appears to pervade so much of the public discourse of late is not occurring within a vacuum. There are certainly the cases of Oklahoma's attempts to ban the consideration of sharia law from its courts system; attempts in over a dozen other states to block the construction of mosques and Islamic community centers; and a general antipathy leveled towards Muslims in some quarters. These are some of the several social currents concerning highly contestable and controversial issues. Arizona and Alabama have passed measures aimed at limiting illegal immigration; while this is understandable for the former as a border state, it is puzzling for the latter which lacks a foreign land neighbor. These measures are seen as being less than veiled measures to racially profile people of color and the scope of the laws will doubtless impact upon people who are legal residents and/or citizens, though lacking in "American appearance." Some politicians and advocates for these measures have claimied that in addition to protecting the country's borders from the infiltration of job stealing foreigners, the legislation also helps prevent easy access to terrorists through porous.

The United States Constitution, and in particular the First Amendment, guarantees the right to Americans to practise their respective religions free of unreasonable restrictions from the government. For Muslim Americans, the scope and scale of this right is informed, as it is for other religious minorities, by locating space within a society that, although officially secular, reinforces and preserves the Protestant civil ethos of the current majority population. In other words, America is by default a Protestant Christian country and all other religions navigate the public realm in response to that reality. A simple example of this phenomenon of the majoritarian default is the school calendar - Monday to Friday - with all major Christian holidays built into the calendar. For all other religions, there is an exhaustive process to assert and prove the necessity of allowing a student to be excused without suffering adverse impact or penalty to his/her academic studies for merely taking the day off for, say, Eid observances. When Muslim Americans make efforts to seek similar accommodations and dispensations that have been granted to other groups, they are branded as attempting to implement and impose sharia law upon American society. The term "Creeping Sharia" is invoked for any effort to provide space for Islam within the public sphere. Similarly, efforts to opt out of certain school activities due to religious or cultural sensitivities otherizes Muslim Americans as foreigners and unwilling to assimilate to "American values." In some cases, other religious communities, like Evangelical Christians have demanded exemption from participating in school Halloween activities on religious grounds. School districts have responded by canceling the activities completely. Despite the episode lacking any Muslim involvement, Muslim families have been blamed as the ones who "ruined" a long-standing American tradition, with critics erroneously assuming that it is they who are reflexively and maliciously opposed to such festivities.

Where religious communities have a critical mass within a particular school district, pragmatism prevails in acknowledging the number of students who will be observing a religious holiday. This is a common occurrence in areas with a large Jewish population, where the Jewish high holidays, which occur in the autumn, are presented as a day off for everyone. As Muslims are similarly gaining identifiable population concentrations, such practical considerations are being made. In 2015, the New York City public school district, the largest school district in the country, recognized both Eid festivals as official holidays in the school calendar. (Gyrnbaum, 2015)

American football is more than the national pastime; it is firmly ensconced as part of the nation's civil religion. The annual Super Bowl championship match for professional football takes on a quasi-sacred atmosphere when the game is played on a Sunday in early February. The sport is very popular both at the collegiate and high school levels as well. At Dearborn Fordson High School in Dearborn, Michigan, the student population is 90% Arab Muslim. In 2011, Ramadan occurred during the summer months, prime time for football practice prior to the season beginning in September. Most of the football players on the Fordson team were Muslim, and were faced with 17-hour fasts on hot summer days in which to conduct their grueling practice regimens. Coach Fouad Zaban consulted his team, who all agreed unanimously to move the practice sessions to nighttime, after the Muslim players had the opportunity to break their fasts, get rehydrated and be able to escape the sun and heat of the day. (Longman, 2011) Such solutions to issues are hardly an example of imposing sharia upon an unsuspecting population. Yet, the goodwill exhibited at Fordson High School along with the fact that Dearborn has the highest concentration of Arabs outside the Middle East, was sufficient enough for former Louisiana Governor and Indian-American Piyush "Bobby" Jindal to claim that Dearborn was one of a few cities in America that were "no-go" zones for non-Muslims because they were hostile to anyone not practising Islam, due in large part to their purported implementation of sharia law. This canard was vehemently denied by Dearborn's mayor, John O'Reilly, an Irish Catholic, yet despite such assertions and despite overwhelming evidence to the contrary, Jindal refused to retract his obvious and bigoted lie. (Graham, 2015) One could reasonably imply that Amish communities and several Christian communities throughout the so-called "Bible Belt" are far more fitting of Jindal's description of exclusivist, unwelcoming communities that apply a community social contract based upon their own religious values irrespective of whether they are inimical to the US Constitution.

Perhaps the biggest concern facing the Muslim American community is the American Muslim community faces the challenge of being defined by external forces, whether by non-Muslims in the country or by Muslims outside the United States. After all, it is by far the most diverse collective in the Islamic world, with every conceivable ethnicity, race, language family, culture and doctrinal persuasion represented in a pastiche replicated only during the Hajj for ten days annually. It is also, in relative terms, one of the youngest Muslim communities on earth, with a presence spanning four centuries, but in measurable terms, a little more than a hundred years. The diffuse nature of the community, coupled with its veritable "youth," allow for tremendous opportunity in shaping its identity, provided the mechanics and challenges of doing so are realized. Is there such a thing as an American Muslim identity? If so, what does it look like and if not, is it attainable? These questions may each be answered in the affirmative; however, the subsequent inquiry as to its composition and characteristics is decidedly a work in progress.

Identity construction is a function of three "A's:" agency, authenticity and authority, irrespective of whether a fourth "A," assimilation, is an objective for a community. Contrary to a popular conceit, identity is not merely a passive phenomenon; it requires a constant process of engagement, contestation and negotiation, as identity requires evolution. Adding another layer of complexity, and particularly in the American context, there is no absence of effort by people outside the Muslim community to define it, often in pejorative, anti-social and even dangerous terminology. Whether as a reaction to such efforts or as an affirmative imperative, Muslims need to be agents of their own narrative and must therefore actively shape and define their identity.

While all Muslims have the ability and right to play an active role in shaping the contours of American Muslim identity, the issue of authenticity often militates against such participation occurring easily. While the diversity of the community in the United States is a tremendous asset, it has also been a source of discord as different subgroups attempt to dominate the definition of being Muslim. This may occur across such tectonic plates as immigrant/indigenous lines, sectarian difference or even longevity of being Muslim. Of course, there are certain doctrinal criteria that constitute a sine qua non for being Muslim; however, cultural, racial and ethnic factors sometimes become additional, artificial barriers to contributing to an American Muslim identity construction.

Related to the issue of authenticity is authority: who can legitimately participate in the process of defining Muslims? Unfortunately, the same factors that inform discussions on authenticity permeate into notions of authority. While some will assert that only a particular notion of piety can qualify one to define the Muslim community, a more common, tacit demand occurs when people conflate religion with culture or even ethnicity. Equally pernicious is the potential for socio-economic factors to become a mode of exclusion to the venues where communal identity is discussed, deliberated and defined.

The development of identity may be an imperative for those seeking to define themselves, but a key component of how American Muslims perceive themselves is how and where they situate the location of the United States within the broader Muslim world. Certain theological realities place the consciousness of Muslims and their piety upon Mecca, this making the city a natural center for Islam. In doing so, and given its geographic distance, America becomes the periphery relative to the Arabian core. American Muslims of immigrant or indigenous heritage alike may share such a conception. But while Mecca orients Muslims toward it liturgically, other factors affect religious identity beyond the theological. Clearly, the culture, language, even Islamic doctrine of Western Arabia is not essentialised across the Muslim world; Muslims in Southeast Asia and Africa, for example, maintain their own cultural lens through which their practice of Islam is refracted. While the Hijaz may be a religious epicenter, it is not necessarily a cultural core. American Muslims have the ability to develop their own modalities of religious identity through the appropriation of domestic cultural markers that are in accordance with Islamic sensibilities. In doing so, they will be emulating their coreligionists in other parts of the world and from other historical periods, since Islam, qua religion, was able to assume the cultural paradigm, by and large, in which it expanded.

American Muslims, like other ethno-cultural and religious groups in the United States, are already involved in the dynamic endeavor of developing their identity. While many do so as an extension of their ontology as Muslims, others construct a sense of self and community as a reaction to dominant culture and/or negative aspersions cast upon Islam or Muslims locally and abroad. While Muslims face the challenge of others defining the community, often in contravention to their own efforts and constructions, they also have to resist the importation or imposition of foreign modalities of identity, especially when such characteristics militate against practical or desired application. As Muslims in the United States carve out their own place within the country's social and cultural landscape, they do so by concomitantly forging their unique position within the Muslim world as well. At the same time, they have had to confront an ever increasingly toxic public sphere that demonizes Islam and Muslims with impunity.

To explain why anti-Muslim rhetoric appears to be stronger now than even after 9-11, perhaps a more significant date is not 2001, but 2007. In that year, the Pew Center for the Study of Religious Life published an extensive report on Muslims in America. Among the hundreds of pages of data, one statistic gained considerable attention. The report placed the Muslim population in this country at roughly 2.35 million, dramatically lower than the previously and oft-cited estimate of 6 to 8 million people. (Pew Research Center, 2007) Instead of Islam being the second largest religion in America, at about three percent of the population, the new figures placed the community at less than one percent of society. While this steep reduction in numbers could be interpreted to allay fears about the "Muslim threat" in the nation, a second approach was taken. As the Muslim population is much smaller than previously believed, it is barely more than a statistical anomaly, incapable of being taken seriously or affecting public or political opinion. Almost immediately, an amplified negative discourse began in the public sphere, among media and political elites now emboldened to speak in terms about Muslims that they would not dare to use about other groups in the country. As the 2008 elections approached, the Muslim community vacillated between being a pariah and a threat, to be avoided at all costs by those seeking election to office. No major candidate for president wished to be seen at a Muslim sponsored event and several were wary of accepting Muslim donations lest they received unwanted scrutiny in the media. Though some may have anticipated such anti-Muslim fervor to be ephemeral, limited only to the election cycle of 2008, the hostility continued beyond inauguration day in 2009 as many of the same issues in the culture wars remained and even increased. If the cultural sands of America are shifting more than what is acceptable for some people by virtue of the transformations of ethnic and social mores, the election of the first African American president in 2008 was seen as a significant change for the nation. While some were inspired by Barack Obama's ascendancy to the country's highest elected office and believed it was evidence that America had moved beyond its difficult racial history, it was not a universally held sentiment. Racism, which may have been latent in many quarters, manifested itself in subtle or tangential ways. The President was questioned about his faith, whether he was a Muslim, and about his eligibility to be president by questioning whether he was in fact an American, or a Kenyan. In both instances, there was a concerted campaign to portray the President as being alien, a foreigner, someone ineligible to serve as Commander in Chief. Of course, his biography is a matter of public record and scrutiny, incontrovertibly stating that he was born in Honolulu, Hawai'i (the year after it was admitted into the Union) and is a Christian (despite having an atheist father of Muslim heritage and belonging to a congregation in Chicago whose pastor gained controversy and notoriety).

The contestation of the President's biographical bona fides may have been resolved, though not for some who stubbornly deny evidence supporting his assertions. Notwithstanding the public debates surrounding the issue, the use of religious and national origin tropes reveals much about the moral panic that possesses Obama's detractors. The issue of racial bigotry, though still evident, has become sufficiently stigmatised that open aspersions and attacks based on race are no longer tolerated. In today's culture-speak, one would never deign to call the President using the "N" word; instead, anger at the first African American president could be discharged by accusing him of being the "M" word, i.e. "Muslim." The xenophobia driving this phenomenon had two functions: impugn the president under the cover of a transferred cultural trope (i.e. Muslim) and to disparage members of this group, genuine or otherwise, with impunity. In a sense, and despite the invocation of religious tropes such as sharia and "stealth jihad," current debates imply the racialization of Muslims, subjecting them to a discourse very similar to African Americans in the civil rights era and similar aspersions against Catholics and Jews at earlier stages of American history.

As the morphology of America changes with ethnic shifts

toward a larger Hispanic presence and culture, the redefinition of marriage and the dismantling of racial homogeneity in the country's leadership, Americans have also been saddled with uncertainties regarding the economy as well as the nation's previously presumed dominance on the international stage. With emerging economic powers such as China, India, Russia and Brazil, the prospect of the United States declining so rapidly from being the world's sole superpower to one nation among many is a frightening, demoralizing prospect. Clearly, anger cannot be directed against other countries, especially those that are asserting new conventions of strength. Similarly, on the domestic front, many of the suspect groups seen as driving the most dramatic social and cultural shifts are beyond direct and open reproach given their perceived strength politically, financially and historically. The only community remaining in America that is the object of derision and lacks social and political capital is the Muslim American population. As a result, the anger and hostility leveled against it may appear to be disproportionate to its size unless one assesses such attitudes as being vicariously channeled toward it in lieu of their actual intended targets.

Of late, there has been a coalescence of various demographic shifts in the United States, culminating in the emergence of a new moral panic, where deep rooted fears of a significant, irreversible change in the social order is imminent. Spasms of such an anxiety have been present for some time - some may argue for at least the last several decades since the turbulence of the 1960's - but the intensification of these concerns appears to be related to the impending paradigm change in American demographics estimated for the year 2050. (Beutel & Khan, 2014) Midway through this century, the United States is scheduled to become a majority minority nation. For some, this is a source for considerable consternation as it brings with it simultaneously the end of an era perceived to be a permanent part of the American experience and also the sense of uncertainty and possible foreboding of an America which may not readily be recognizable to them. Muslim Americans find themselves within the maelstrom of a changing social, cultural and political landscape, combatting xenophobia and securitization while striving to maintain Islamic identity and with themselves as a positive, contributory and safe demographic.

Consequently, the bigotry faced by Muslim Americans is an example of the epistemic racism that exists in the United States and is now being deployed by a majority population that is fearful of what the potential erosion of its cultural domination, its white, Christian, straight male privilege and its hegemonic power portends. Such rhetoric, and its validation by official government actors, is prima facie evidence of the rampant institutionalized racism that has been a feature of the American civic landscape for centuries, and that is now manifesting itself against Muslim Americans. (Grosfoguel, 2010) The Islamophobia Studies Center, located at the University of California, Berkeley, is one a few academic and non-academic affiliated organizations that chronicles and maps the pervasive scope and scale of anti-Muslim hatred in the United States, including its connections to institutionalized racism.

The Ummah is a very powerful concept of identity and belonging. For Muslim Americans, being part of the global Muslim community is a critical engagement that keeps it connected with the rest of the Muslim world, whether through family or ancestral ties or a deep sense of connectivity with the fraternity of fellow religionists, especially as the United States is on the periphery of the so-called Muslim world. As such, Muslim Americans pay attention to the conditions of Muslims in various parts of the world, especially those communities that are in dire circumstances. Certain conflicts, like the Palestinian issue or Kashmir maintain a perpetual level of focus for the Muslim community, while others appear when an acute or exigent situation arises, whether a natural disaster or a manmade crisis.

Regarding the Palestinian issue, the Muslim American community has devoted considerable effort and resources to highlight the plight of Palestinians while countering political efforts that further prejudice or adversely affect them. The latest expression of demonstrating solidarity with the Palestinians for many Muslim Americans is subscription to the Boycott, Divestment, Sanctions (BDS) Movement, the initiative of Palestinian civil society to exert pressure on Israel to ostensibly end the occupation, or at the least, alleviate the suppression of the Palestinian territories. The movement has gained considerable momentum on college campuses as well as among Muslim communities across the country as boycotts are a time-honoured aspect of American social activism. At the same time, opposition to the BDS movement has grown and has attempted to reframe the issue as a targeted act of bigotry singling out Israel for criticism, even accusing BDS supporters of anti-Semitism. American politicians have tried to rebut the effects of BDS by proposing legislation that makes compliance with BDS a criminal act. Of course, such laws run the risk of violating the US Constitution and its First Amendment protections as a boycott is deemed to be an expression of political speech, the most protected form of speech in US law. At the same time, some within the Muslim community regard BDS as an obligatory imperative for Muslim Americans, the bare minimum that can be done to show solidarity with the Palestinian cause; failure to do so is tantamount to heresy.

The BDS issue has been recently deployed to label Muslim politicians like Congresswomen Rashida Tlaib and Ilhan Omar as anti-Semites for their consistent and vocal support for the BDS movement. It will doubtless be invoked during the 2020 reelection campaigns against both women as political opponents will seek to exploit differences by weaponizing the Israel-Palestine conflict for political gain. Despite efforts to categorize the BDS movement as an anti-Semitic Muslim project, BDS has gained support among non-Muslims, including the Presbyterian and Quaker Churches as well as Jewish Voice for Peace (JVP), an organization that opposes anti-Jewish, anti-Muslim and anti-Arab bigotry. Organizations like American Muslims for Palestine (AMP), established in 2006 to promote and advocate for the Palestinian narrative and Palestinian rights, have collaborated closely with these churches and JVP to advance the Palestinian cause in the United States, on college campuses, in the media and within civil society.

As with Palestine, Kashmir holds a prominent place in the consciousness and conscience of a large segment of the Muslim American community. Of late, the actions of the Hindu fascist government of the BJP leader Narendra Modi in India has cast a broad spotlight on the plight of Kashmiri Muslims as well as Indian Muslims as a larger group under tremendous pressure. While some may have perceived Kashmir earlier as primarily a South Asian concern, it is an issue that has been internalized by a broader sector of the Muslim American community. In fact, the narratives of Kashmir and Palestine, both being the result of settler colonialism, has created a syncretic space for activism and awareness development on the two issues.

The Muslim American community has endeavored to raise awareness and to seek government intervention on other Muslim crises, such as the Rohingya conflict as well as the suspected ethnic cleansing campaign against the Uyghur in China. The community has also leveraged its resources by collecting and sending humanitarian aid where possible, including trying to remedy the refugee crisis caused by the Syrian conflict since 2011. In fact, the chaos caused by the ongoing turmoil in Syria has been one of the most deeply felt of the various Muslim calamities worldwide and arguably one of the most divisive for Muslims in the United States, particular for Arab communities.

While the Syrian conflict is primarily an issue of a political nature, whereby an authoritarian ruler has attempted to clamp down on dissent within his country, the conflict has taken on broader regional dimensions. Syria became the battleground for the broader proxy war between Saudi Arabia and various Gulf states and Iran. The conflict quickly and reductively became rebranded as another purported example of sectarian animus between Sunni and Shi'i forces. This denominational binary began to dominate the discourse about the conflict among Muslim Americans. Consequently, an objective, measured understanding, as well as the requisite level of empathy for innocent civilians caught in the crossfire of the war, became elusive, if not extinct values within the debates on this issue.

While the Syrian conflict has had a polarising effect along sectarian lines in the United States, the sense of anger and resentment it has created has not reached a level where the sectarianism has reached an insurmountable impasse or descended into violence. At the same time, the identity politics of Islamic sectarianism have assumed a superficial nature in many quarters that makes the presumption of unity a nebulous concept. Such constructions of identity also have the inadvertent effect of compelling many Muslim Americans into taking a side in the conflict, instead of maintaining some modicum of impartiality.

To be fair, however, confessional politics in the Muslim context is hardly a new or American created phenomenon, especially given the history of the modern Middle East. Within the United States, the 2003 invasion of Iraq exacerbated and inflamed latent sectarian divisions. In the lead-up to the 2003 US invasion to oust Saddam Hussein, American officials actively courted support from the Iraqi Shi'i and Christian communities, respectively. Representatives of the George W. Bush administration met with leaders of both factions, under the pretense that both groups had suffered immensely under Hussein's regime and would welcome an American effort to depose him from power. Likewise, the Bush administration ignored categorically the Iraqi Sunni community, presuming that it would at best be ambivalent, and at worst actively oppose the second Gulf War. The contrast in treatment by Washington of the two respective Muslim communities created some ill feelings, particularly because of the mistrust it engendered. Shi'i Iraqis thought that Iraqi Sunni opposition to the invasion was tantamount to explicit support for Saddam, while Sunnis dreaded the prospect of a power vacuum or disenfranchisement and discrimination if the Shi'i were to gain power in a post-Hussein Iraq.

After the fall of Baghdad in April 2003, many Iraqi Shi'i in America were jubilant, while Sunnis were muted and pensive. However, after the fall of Fallujah in 2004 and the ensuing chaos and outbreak of civil war that followed, both denominations were feeling the sense of disarray over a country in shambles.

Foreign focus by the Muslim American community is understandable and natural. After all, the population of Muslims in the United States is less than 0.2% of the Ummah. But the attention paid to the broader Muslim world does carry with it some opportunity costs domestically. The American Muslim community, according to national surveys, reflects broader social trends, with the majority of its population being part of the country's middle class. Its diversity translates into a wide spectrum of socio-economic realities, and while there is some tremendous affluence, there is considerable privation as well, especially within inner city communities. As previously stated, some of the socio-economic divides are also informed by a strong racial component. Family and country ties, as well as significant media awareness and attention placed upon foreign conflicts, creates the conditions for Muslim Americans, especially those of immigrant backgrounds, to send charity and humanitarian aid overseas. Often, this occurs at the expense and to the detriment, if not complete ignorance, of the needs of Muslims within their own local environs. Such dynamics create resentment and tension within the Muslim community as ethno-racial bias, whether conscious or not, manifests itself in decisions over to where to send funds and help causes. Worse, when wealthy Muslims come to the aid of their co-religionists in the United States, they may encounter accusations of being patronizing and condescending in considering fellow Americans to be of secondary importance. This process of inferiorization may not be intentional but may evoke negative sentiments from recipients.

Muslim Americans are hardly unique in the struggle to reconcile the global with the local. With its relatively small population, the community is essentially an outlier compared to the critical mass of Muslims located in Africa and Asia. It is understandable that so much attention will be placed upon those locales where Muslims are embroiled in conflicts and face destitution. Yet, sometimes, the imperative to focus on the foreign creates fissures within the Muslim American landscape. For those Muslims who are either non-immigrant or perhaps second, third generation or older, their consciousness may be inclined more to the domestic than to the global. They have difficulty relating, either because of language or cultural barriers, to the context and significance of issues occurring in some far off place that they have neither visited nor studied. They may feel coerced into caring about a conflict that they don't understand just to conform to the dictates of stronger advocates, relegating matters that may concern them more directly and imminently. Ironically, for immigrant Muslim Americans, this dynamic was on full display in the aftermath of 9-11. Many were confronted, for the first time, with the realization that their civil liberties had been eroded by the USA Patriot Act and the securitization of the community. Muslim Americans could no longer enjoy the presumption of innocence and immunity from suspicion simply for striving to achieve and live the "American dream" of a suburban, middle-class, gentrified lifestyle. It is no coincidence that the vast majority of advocacy organizations and political activism that places its focus on the domestic, not the overseas Muslim community, occurred after 2001 although the need to prepare and act prophylactically had always existed.

The USA Patriot Act was a hallmark of the George W. Bush administration's efforts to impose a broad and deep system of securitization on the Muslim American community, although the structures and mechanisms of the policy remain intact and apply to society at large. Muslim Americans served as the proverbial "canaries in the coalmine," the experimental target community to assess how far society would accept the erosion of civil rights and civil liberties. Apparently, most Americans were comfortable when it appeared the restrictions were limited to just one suspect group, i.e. Muslim Americans. While there was some perceptible protest when it became obvious the security changes were indefinite or permanent, and had a far wider dragnet than previously believed, no significant opposition has been mounted to reexamine, let alone repeal the measures. If anything, such restrictions have become further institutionalized to combat the so-called "War on Terror."

While the Bush "43" presidency is credited with the USA Patriot Act and the institutional expansion of government encroachment on civil liberties through the creation of the massive Department of Homeland Security, the issue of securitization is a bipartisan imperative. On December 31, 2011, President Barack Obama signed into law the National Defense Authorization Act for Fiscal Year 2012. Although President Obama included a signed statement in which he expressed concerns about the law's scope and potential for adverse impact on American citizens, he nonetheless enabled its enactment, complete with some highly troublesome provisions. The NDAA allows for indefinite detention, even of US citizens, and for detention without trial, ostensibly, a clear violation of the US Constitution and its protections of due process rights. In addition, the NDAA sanctions military custody. Of course, this would allow for the continuing use of facilities like Guantanamo Bay, a detention center that then candidate Obama had pledged to close once elected.

The scholar, author and civil rights activist W.E.B. DuBois once challenged his African American community with the question, "How does it feel to be a problem?" as a way to make them think about how society had problematized them as the cause, instead of the victims, of racial tensions in America. (DuBois, 1903) The same inquiry may apply to the Muslim American community, especially after the 9-11 attacks, where Muslims are made to be a collective problem, if not a collective threat to the country. This stigmatization, like that within the African American community when DuBois posed the question, has become internalized by large segments of the Muslim American community, particularly by those young Muslims who came of age after the 9-11 attacks, and may have no memory of a world for Muslim Americans before the paradigm shift occurred.

Of course, the problematization of Muslims in the United States is nothing new, and the arc of internalization predates 9-11. The 1993 World Trade Center attack created a sentiment of foreboding for Muslim Americans who began to internalize any and all acts of mass murder and/or terrorism as being potentially caused by Muslims; this was a function of media and government statements, both implicit and explicit. Both institutions intimated at the possibility that the 1995 Oklahoma City terrorist attack on a federal office building could have been perpetrated by Muslims before it was substantiated that the attack was committed by a white, right wing terrorist, Timothy McVeigh. Similarly, FBI officials attempted to force the narrative of possible Muslim involvement in the 1996 TWA Flight 800 tragedy, where a Boeing 747 exploded shortly after departure from New York's JFK International Airport. A faulty fuel tank was proved to be the cause of that incident, though no retraction or admission of error was ever offered by the government for its defamatory impugnment of an entire community. As a result, Muslim Americans developed a strange but understandable reaction to any act of violence reported by the media. They would react with the common supplication of, "Please God, don't let it be a Muslim who did it." Muslim Americans had bought into the narrative constructed about them that they were presumptively the perpetrators, guilty unless proven otherwise.

Muslim Americans have become privy to a near daily supply of images and rhetoric that generally casts Islam and Muslims in a negative light. As political writer and researcher Arun Kundnani has stated, "Neoconservatives invented the terror war, but Obama's liberalism normalized it, at which point, mainstream journalists stopped asking questions" (Kundnani, 2014). The role of journalists as a menace and threat to the nation, along with ideologically driven policy makers and a zealous government apparatus completes the troika of forces that have constructed the *golem* of the Muslim American, an unnatural, unhuman creature of fear.

A plethora of reports and scholarly articles confirm that coverage of Islam and Muslims is overwhelmingly and disproportionately negative compared to similar coverage of other religious groups. In many cases, the religious affiliation of a Muslim actor is mentioned in the news report irrespective of whether it bears any relevance to the underlying story. No such reflexive reference is made for non-Muslims. In addition, media accounts appear to presume that any act of violence committed by a Muslim must be motivated by some religious imprimatur and is therefore labeled as an act of terrorism. Again, no such presumption is made for any other religionist, no matter how egregious the crime and sometimes, despite the explicit proclamations of religious motivation made by the individual in question. Similarly, while a Muslim suspect is invariably reduced to a caricature of a religiously fanatical automaton, the non-Muslim suspect will enjoy the benefit of a deep analysis into his/her psyche to assess whether he/she was mentally disturbed and will delve into possible causes of abuse or dysfunctionality in his/her background. And then, of course, there is the "T" word. Until only very recently, media accounts were loathe to invoke the term, terrorism, for any of acts of violence committed by a non-Muslim, irrespective of the political motivation, stated intent to terrorize or aftermath. A cottage industry of punditry brought a host of so-called experts, most with no cultural or scholarly experience regarding Islam, Muslims or even geopolitics, on air to discuss why any act of violence had to have Muslim fingerprints behind it. Media, politicians and government officials were reluctant even to acknowledge the existence of domestic terrorist threats that did not involve Muslim suspects. As a result, billions of dollars were expended to combat a non-existent threat, while official policy ignored, and perhaps concealed, the far greater threat of white supremacist based domestic terrorism. Only recently, essentially since the election of Donald Trump in 2016 and the far more blatant and frequent violent acts of white supremacists, have opinion makers and politicians begun to expand the scope of the usage of the word, terrorism, albeit still begrudgingly and apprehensively. Cynically, it appears that media outlets and politicians are only now willing to attribute the term to non-Muslim American actors because they seek to connect President Trump's toxic rhetoric to the white supremacist movement and suggest that he is normalizing, if not enabling domestic terrorism.

Such selective use of terminology and its deployment for the sake of convenience, expediency and profit is not lost on Muslim Americans, who have endured demonization and defamation within the public discourse as a default position for decades. While they have become inured to its consistency, it is the consequences that are of particular concern for the community, as the hate-filled rhetoric now emanates from the White House, giving cover and encouragement to those in civil society to follow suit with impunity, and perhaps infer that they can act upon their bigoted impulses. There has been a steady increase in anti-Muslim hate crimes since 9-11, with a sharp escalation in the first three years of the Trump presidency. Women being assaulted for wearing the hijab has become a common occurrence, leading to death in some cases. Similarly, identifiably Muslim spaces have now come under threat, either by menacing behavior, including hate mail and threatening messages left on mosque answering machines, to stalking of mosques and Islamic schools. These buildings, as well as private homes of Muslim Americans, have been the targets of vandalism, profane graffiti as well as destruction of property and even arson. Some mosques and Islamic schools have even been the targets of gunfire and explosive devices, at times when congregants have been present for worship or other activities.

The xenophobia that is trafficked from the highest levels of government today has left many Muslim Americans anxious about their future in the country. President Trump has taken to social media to excoriate Congresswomen Omar and Tlaib for their criticism of his policies by responding that if they don't like it here, they can "go home." (Ygliesias, 2019) Tlaib was in fact born in Detroit, Michigan and is therefore a natural born US citizen, while Omar arrived as a refugee at the age of ten and became a naturalized US citizen when she was seventeen. Trump's brazen retorts affirm the sentiment held by many Muslim Americans, especially those of immigrant background, that they will always be seen as inauthentic, disloyal Americans who have to constantly prove their allegiance as American bona fides, while facing taunts to leave even if they are simply exercising that very American trait of political protest that the majority population enjoys as a matter of course. For the vast majority of Muslims Americans, who have crossed the proverbial Rubicon when they came to the United States, such taunts, while offensive, hurtful and potentially dangerous if not challenged and checked, America is home and it is their only viable home. Out of a sense of defiance or simply an expression of American obstinance, they have determined to defy the anti-Muslim fervor, taking lessons from communities who similarly had to run the gauntlet of American acceptance to establish a quintessentially American version of Islam and a Muslim community with its own complex identity and ethos.

Chapter 3

Overview of Islamophobia and Racism in Chicago and Detroit

Chicago

Chicago goes by many monikers- the Windy City, the Second City (due to its being the second largest American city to New York, before its relegation to third by Los Angeles in the mid-20th century). Thanks to its proximity to the Great Plains and the Great Lakes regions, Chicago is a formidable hub for transportation, commerce, finance, industry, technology and telecommunications. It is headquarters to several of America's largest corporations, including McDonald's, Boeing, Kraft Heinz and Allstate Insurance. It is also home to one of the largest Muslim communities in the United States. It is a community that has roots dating back well over a century.

One of the earliest Muslim communities in Chicago came from the former Ottoman Empire. The Bosnians, along with Arabs and African Americans established Muslim organizations well before the mass influx of Muslim immigrants that began arriving in the mid 1960s and beyond. The Bosnians established the Muslimansko Potpomagajuce Drustvo Dzemijetul in 1906 as a mutual aid and benevolent society. It is considered to be the oldest Muslim organization in America. The Bosnian Muslim community established a mosque within Chicago city limits in 1957, but subsequently relocated to the northern suburb of Northbrook in the 1970s. The Islamic Cultural Center of Chicago has a multi-ethnic congregation and a building with Bosnian architecture and a Bosnian Imam. The facility also houses a school and a cultural center. (Puskar, 2007)

In the early 1900s, Arab Muslims from Palestine began to arrive in the Chicago area. They settled in the city's South Side, close to the African-American community, as small business owners. Their population grew after World War II and the ensuing chaos brought about by the end of the British mandate in Palestine and the creation of the state of Israel in 1948. Arab Muslims established the city's first Arab mosque in 1954 as the Mosque Foundation. It re-located in 1982 to the south west suburb of Bridgeview as the community expanded and sought life away from the inner city. Today, the Mosque Foundation is one of the largest Islamic centers in the Chicago area and houses two full-time accredited schools. (Cainkar, 2009)

A critical component of Muslim American life in Chicago is the African American Muslim community. The Nation of Islam relocated to Chicago in 1934 from Detroit, where it had been founded by W.D. Fard. After Fard mysteriously disappeared, Elijah Muhammad took over the ministry and moved the congregation to Chicago, establishing Temple #2 in the city's South Side. He also established the Muhammad University of Islam, which is still a functioning institution. (GhaneaBassiri, 2010) Muhammad preached a message of black empowerment, at times, even black superiority, along with self-sufficiency and spiritual growth for Black Americans. The Nation of Islam ensured that the neighborhood in which their facilities were located would be free of crime, blight and anti-social behavior. It empowered and enabled black owned businesses to create a self-contained, thriving social and religious ecosystem. The South Side of Chicago around Temple #2 became the place where cultural icon and heavyweight boxing champion Muhammad Ali gained his Muslim consciousness, shedding his former Christian identity of Cassius Clay, developing his Islamic faith and observance. He benefited from being at the Nation's headquarters where Rev. Muhammad was based and where Malcolm X was a frequent visitor. Upon Elijah Muhammad's death in 1975, the ministry first passed to his son, Wallace (Warith Deen, or W.D.) Muhammad. However, within a decade, W.D. Muhammad took nearly 90% of the Nation's congregation into mainstream Sunni Islam. The remaining membership of the Nation, along with its facilities, were subsequently led by Minister Louis Farrakhan. (GhaneaBassiri, 2010)

Following the relaxation of immigration quotas in the mid 1960s, Chicago became a destination for a significant influx of Muslims from many parts of the world, especially South Asia. Large numbers of Indians and Pakistanis arrived in the midwestern city, drawn by the prospects of job opportunities as well as the process of chain migration, i.e. knowledge of an already established community or family arrival in earlier waves. In 1969, the South Asian immigrants established the MCC, Muslim Community Center, within the city and it is one of Chicago's oldest mosques. Because of its cultural focus well placed on South Asian customs, traditions and language, the MCC became a magnet for Chicago's "Indo-Pak" community, most of whom were scattered across the various suburban areas. Programming, including a weekend school and regularly scheduled social dinners and religious functions like weddings, expanded to develop a full-time school. (www.mcccchicago.org) As communities have now grown, particularly in the suburbs, new centers have opened that cater to Muslims seeking the convenience of proximity, both for worship as well as social and educational needs.

The Muslim American community of Chicago has been well established for well over a century. There are an estimated 400,000 Muslims in the metropolitan area, with a diversity reflective of the broader Muslim world. (www.cairchicago.org) At the same time, it is a community that has faced the challenges and vitriol of Islamophobia and securitization. While some might infer that both have been a post-9-11 phenomenon, evidence suggests that segments of the Chicago area Muslim community started to be targeted by the US government at least two decades prior to the terrorist attacks.

Bridgeview, Illinois is a middle-class suburb, located 15 miles southwest of downtown Chicago. It has been home to the Mosque Foundation, a center that was originally established by Arab Palestinians on Chicago's South Side, since the 1950s. A move to the suburbs is often regarded as being a quintessentially American example, and goal, of upward mobility and success in attaining the "American Dream." But for the Bridgeview Muslim community, there was the pernicious, yet unknown reality that it had been under state surveillance since the 1980s, with an intensification of such policies during the 1990s and 2000s. It is important to highlight that to date, no one from the Bridgeview community has been charged with the crime of terrorism. Despite that fact, individuals as well as the Muslims associated with the Mosque Foundation were watched, stalked, had their homes and mosque wiretapped and were subject to a dragnet the extent of which remains undetermined. (Cainkar, 2009)

The surveillance of the Bridgeview Muslim community began in an era where its Islamic affiliation was one of several factors that placed them under suspicion of government officials. The fact that the community was predominantly Palestinian appears to be the real reason that the surveillance program was initiated in the mid-1980s, which coincided with the emergence of

HAMAS and increased activity of the Palestine Liberation Organization as well as various terrorist acts committed by its affiliates. In 1985, the Achille Lauro cruise ship was hijacked by members of the Palestine Liberation Front. One hostage was killed, and the incident received international coverage. In the same year, TWA Flight 847 was hijacked after take-off from Cairo en route to Athens, and was directed to landed in Beirut with 147 passengers and crew on board. The hostages were released after being held for two weeks, with one passenger, a US Navy diver, being killed. Both incidents occurred against the backdrop of the Lebanese Civil War, the 1982 Israeli invasion of southern Lebanon, the Sabra-Shatilla Massacre and the 1983 bombing of the US Marine barracks in Beirut. (Cainkar, 2009) The fact that American personnel and entities were involved placed the Palestinian community in the United States under scrutiny by government officials who were alerted by Israeli intelligence of possible ties between Palestinian Americans and the various Palestinian entities suspected of being behind the attacks of 1985. The coordination between American and Israeli authorities to spy on American citizens in the United States confirmed what many Arabs and Muslims had suspected about the collaborative and cooperative relationship between the two governments despite raising significant and alarming questions of violations of civil liberties and constitutional protections of due process.

In 1993, Mohammad Salah, a naturalized US citizen of Palestinian origin, was arrested in Israel during a humanitarian visit to the Gaza. He was charged with lending material support to HAMAS, a fairly nebulous and wide ranging indictment whose scope of activities is arbitrary and poorly specified. The Israelis claim Salah signed a confession, though he maintains that it was obtained via torture. Salah was released in 1998, after five years in Israeli detention, and returned to his home in Bridgeview. Six years later, Salah was indicted by American federal prosecutors on the same charges he had received while in Israel. The United States Department of State had designated HAMAS to be a terrorist organization in 1993, the very same year Salah had traveled to Gaza, and the same year he was indicted in Israel. Strangely, the US authorities did not pursue any prosecution against him until 2004, eleven years after the original charges had been filed in Israel and six years after his return to the United States. Salah was eventually acquitted of the main charge but was convicted of the lesser charge of obstruction of justice, an offense that requires a considerably low threshold of proof to demonstrate guilt. (Misra, 2018)

The theory of how Salah came to the attention of US federal authorities is that Israeli intelligence notified the FBI, which acted upon the information as an impetus and justification to launch its Operation Vulgar Betrayal program, a federal investigation tracking and seizing alleged Middle Eastern terrorist funds. The program was also designed to apprehend American citizens who were purportedly supplying monies to Palestinian entities. Operation Vulgar Betrayal was launched by the FBI Chicago field Office in 1996. It closed in 2000 after the prosecutor failed to bring any charges under its mandate. The program was resurrected in 2002, after 9-11, before closing once again in 2007. (Misra, 2018)

The true extent of surveillance tactics and targets for the Bridgeview Muslim community has required considerable legal and investigative effort to uncover. Filmmaker and documentarian Assra Boundaoui, an Algerian-American who at one time lived in the Bridgeview area and was a member of the Mosque Foundation, proceeded to explore the US government's actions on her community. She made several requests to the federal agencies to release documents pertaining to the issue by way of the Freedom of Information Act. She was successful in obtaining over 30,000 documents after significant legal proceedings and notwithstanding government defiance to release them. Despite receiving such a large cache of evidence, it is unknown what percentage it represents of the overall trove regarding the matter. Even the documents she did receive were nonetheless heavily edited; over 70% were in fact redacted. (Misra, 2018)

What Boundaoui discovered confirmed the community's and her own worst suspicions, that the federal government - her own government - had been involved in a multi-year, multi-faceted surveillance campaign against private citizens and Muslim institutions. The documents revealed explicit monitoring of homes, community centers, even Muslim schools, under the guise of finding purported links to terrorism. All of this was done without sufficient probable cause and was an excessively wide net to retrieve information with the vast majority of it being an abject breach of privacy and civil liberties.

Boundaoui's research corroborated long-held suspicions by Muslim community members in Bridgeview of inexplicable activity. Community residents she interviewed spoke of suspicious installations of smoke detectors in mosques and schools, located in places that defied logic due to their odd placement. They also spoke of routinely hearing clicks while speaking on their telephones and noticing strange cars parked in front of schools, mosques and their homes at bizarre hours of the day and night. People started to notice strange and unfamiliar faces at prayer times at the mosque, with peculiar and proactive conversations as if the new individuals were seeking to elicit incriminating remarks from mosque attendees. Some Muslims suspected both these new faces as well as long-time community members of being government informants who were recording anything that was being said. Many residents had federal agents knocking on their doors, asking invasive questions about their fellow community members, specifically whether they were aware of any particular donations to Muslim charities. (Misra, 2018)

The effect of the suspicious activity occurring in Bridgeview had a chilling effect on the Muslim community. Its members became suspicious of one another. It stifled the otherwise free exchange of communication and had a corrosive effect on community trust. Another consequence was the apprehension many Muslims in Bridgeview felt when it came to discharging their religious obligation to pay *zakat* (alms). Residents were frightened at the prospect of inadvertently and unintentionally donating to a suspect organization or charity lest they came to the attention of the authorities and subject to a possible indictment for lending material support to terrorism.

More recently, another Palestinian American from the Chicago area came under federal scrutiny and an ambitious effort to have her removed from the country. Rasmea Odeh is a well-known Palestinian activist. In 2018, Odeh was stripped of her US citizenship after being in the United States for 23 years. Despite this Odeh was deported to Jordan. Odeh had been arrested in 2013 for "unlawful procurement of naturalization," whereby the federal government accused her of failing to disclose her prior arrest and imprisonment in Israel, in 1969, on alleged terrorism charges. As with the case of Mohammed Salah, Odeh claimed that her confession in Israel was extracted after suffering 25 days of relentless torture and sexual abuse while in Israeli custody. (Crawford, 2018) Her case demonstrated that despite being a model citizen in the United States, her activism for Palestinian causes was sufficient reason for her to be pursued by federal authorities in the United States for a technicality that could lead to her denaturalization, as a result of a coordinated campaign between American officials and a vindictive foreign government.

In essence, the overreaching government surveillance and securitization of Bridgeview made its Muslim community radioactive.

Through her investigative efforts, Boundaoui discovered that the federal authorities had been spying on the Bridgeview community, its institutions and its leaders for possible involvement in terror related activities, including money laundering. (Misra, 2018) Despite all its zeal and intrusiveness, the government was not able to indict a single person for terrorism, but it was not for lack of effort. FBI agents had infiltrated the Bridgeview mosque by attending prayer services for years prior to 9-11. After 2001, the federal authorities simply justified their tactics under the pretense that they were hunting for links between community members and Al Qaeda, Osama bin Laden, Islamic Jihad, as well as Saddam Hussein. For the government, groups and organizations that were diametrically opposed to one another in the Middle East was an irrelevant detail; if it involved Muslims, then some Muslims in Bridgeview must have had ties and were involved in illicit activity.

The collective panic and lack of coherent government policy in the post 9-11 era lead to a blanket program of securitizing Muslim Americans, who were considered to be a collective and imminent threat to national security. The 2001 USA Patriot Act became an easy mechanism by which to monitor entire communities irrespective of whether they violated civil liberties, while providing those who were targeted with little to no legal recourse and at the same time giving government officials near complete immunity from prosecution for their overreach. In March 2003, Ghassan Ballut of the Chicago suburb of Tinley Park was indicted and accused of running the Chicago cell of Palestinian Islamic Jihad. The USA Patriot Act furnished federal authorities with the legal justification and tactics to gather secret evidence against Mr. Ballut. According to the indictment, he was charged with providing "material support" to a foreign terrorist organization and with "financing, extolling, and assisting acts of terror." He was ultimately acquitted of all charges. (Ahmed-Ullah and Cohen, 2003)

Similarly, secret intelligence wire taps were used to develop a case against Khaled Abdul Latif Dumeisi, the publisher of an Arabic language newspaper from Oak Park, Illinois. Mr. Dumeisi was charged with spying on local Ba'ath Party dissidents, on behalf of Saddam Hussein. Mr. Dumesi was sentenced to 46 months in prison on March 31, 2004, for failing to register as a foreign agent, conspiracy, perjury for lying to a federal grand jury and lying before an immigration hearing. Upon serving his sentence, Mr. Dumesi was deported to Jordan. (Bebow, 2004)

The heightened publicity and media spotlight upon the Bridgeview community as a result of the actions of government authorities has led to Muslims in that area to receive threats from the public as well. In January 2015, the Bridgeview mosque received a Facebook threat, targeting the Mosque Foundation. The social media post made specific references to shooting and killing Muslims. Law-enforcement authorities investigated the incident, exposing a certain level of irony given that it was the same agencies' casting of the community in such a negative light that had created the climate for such a threat to be made. The suspect who had posted the Facebook message eventually turned himself in to the authorities but no charges were levelled against him with police explaining that his threats did not carry any serious intent. Apparently, the police were satisfied with his claim and offered no further explanation as to why he would not face charges for such a serious threat.

The Chicago area Muslim community has not been the only target of the overzealous state apparatus in surveilling and placing an entire demographic group under suspicion without cause. Muslims living in America's third largest city, and Illinois as a whole, have also endured various manifestations of Islamophobia and racism. Chicago has a sizable population of Muslim Americans; it is also a very multicultural, cosmopolitan metropolis, that has seen and is home to people from all parts of the world. Yet, despite that fact, Islamophobia is still a reality, dispelling the notion that urban areas somehow are more tolerant due to their diversity. In February 2015, a threatening letter was sent to the Lake in the Hills Mosque, a suburban Islamic center, located less than an hour from Chicago. References were made to bombing people and the mosque, praying for the emergence of another American Civil War, this time with Muslims as the enemy, and seeking the opportunity to shoot "you scum bags." Further excerpts from the letter stated, "we can't wait until it's OK to start bombing you f**kers and your kids so we can reduce the number of slime bags being born in to this world of ours." It went on to say, You, like your radical relatives, serve no purpose on earth. Keep you (sic) eyes open" and, "We are praying for civil war so we can start shooting you slime bags." (DiBenedetto, 2015) Mosque officials alerted law enforcement authorities who investigated the matter but no arrests were made.

There is much to interpret from the statements made in the threatening letter to the Lake in the Hills Mosque. At its most superficial level, it is simply a xenophobic assault on an already suspect and beleaguered American demographic group. Yet, the specificity of the messaging exposes notable textures and thoughts in the sender's mind. The date of the letter, February 2015, is important as it coincides with the emergence and awareness of the egregious activities and attacks of ISIS in the Middle East. American media accounts broadcast images, statements and interviews of people brutalized by the terrorist regime in Iraq and Syria. Incidents reported as domestic terrorism in the United States where Muslims were the alleged perpetrators created both hysteria and a backlash against the Muslim American community. It is reasonable to infer that the author of the letter was acting in accordance with the climate of discourse in the country at a time of heightened panic over ISIS and redirecting his anger back towards Muslim Americans, arguably those living within close proximity.

The fact that the author references "civil war" is particularly noteworthy. It suggests that he or she was already thinking of the United States as being embroiled in a series of binaries. Much of the toxic rhetoric on the Internet and particularly among conservative media outlets has for decades painted America as a nation caught in a massive culture war, blaming liberals, progressives, people of color, feminists, and non-conservative Christians as being behind the destruction of the essential fabric of the country which they believe was, is and should always remain white, Anglo Saxon, Protestant, heterosexual and male dominated. For those who believe that America faces an existential threat from any group that appears to challenge that essentialism, the prospect of a civil war is therefore imminent and perhaps desired. As America moves to become a majority minority nation within the next generation, such invectives reflect the anxiety, despair and hatred at anyone who is seen to represent "the other."

As the Lake of the Hills Mosque letter suggests, Islamophobia is but one facet of a broader moral panic against a myriad of minority demographic groups. The threats of violence are accompanied by an acknowledgment that efforts through legal channels to curb the immigration of foreigners, particularly people of color, or mass deportations are not viable. In addition, this letter was sent in 2015 during the Obama administration. The author was clearly resigned to the reality that the US government would not take action by implementing policies that would mollify his/her xenophobia. This made his/her call for Civil War a matter of "vigilante justice" due to official unwillingness or inability to "solve the problem" of a changing America. Those who share the author's sentiments and perspectives see a civil war and battle against various groups including Muslims as an active patriotism, even national duty. His/her threats to demonize, dehumanize Muslims and warn them and their families to leave the country play well into this narrative of bigotry and hate. Of course, since the 2016 election of Donald Trump, Islamophobes and bigots feel emboldened to speak out in hateful and toxic rhetoric because it merely echoes statements made by the new president, who has normalized and in effect legitimized bigotry from the highest office in the country. Now, Americans, like the author of the threatening letter, have an expectation that the president will lead their charge in the so-called culture war to preserve and protect the current white Anglo-Saxon Protestant majority in perpetuity, and see themselves as his loyal, patriotic foot soldiers to achieve that mission.

Vandalism is a common occurrence in American society. But

generally, suburban communities experience fewer incidents than their stressed counterparts. It was therefore shocking when an act of abject vandalism occurred in the Chicago suburb of Bolingbrook. In May 2019, the home of a Muslim family was attacked with multiple acts of vandalism and intimidation. The family, with six children aged from 2 to 21, had their windows broken and desecrated with anti-Muslim graffiti, homophobic and profanity laden slurs, racial epithets, as well as swastikas painted all over the house's exterior. (CBSChicago, 2019) Local authorities as well as federal agencies investigated the incident as a hate crime.

Islamophobia and anti-Muslim bigotry are not the exclusive province of the disenfranchised and perpetually angry members of a society. As President Trump has demonstrated time and again, it also permeates through the establishment. The Chicago Cubs are one of the few American cities to have two professional baseball teams. Until their World Series victory in 2016, the Cubs held the dubious distinction of being the team with the longest record without a championship, which many fans described as a curse, lasting 71 years. In that time, the Cubs became the city's "lovable losers" and maintained a very loyal and committed fan base. The Cubs have been owned by the Ricketts family since 2009. The patriarch of the family, Joe Ricketts, sent an email in February 2019 contained highly offensive language, including a statement that, Muslims are my (our) enemy." (Sweeney, 2019) Various Chicago area Muslim organizations made public statements condemning the remarks, and demanded action for the Cubs franchise. Ahmed Rehab, Executive Director of the Chicago chapter of the Council on American Relations (CAIR), the Council of Islamic Organizations of Greater Chicago (CIOGC) and the Illinois Muslim Civic Coalition all expressed their dismay and outrage at the unnecessary disparagement of the Muslim community and reminded the Cubs and the public of the number of "long-suffering" Muslim fans that the team had and the unwavering loyalty they demonstrated, especially during the Cubs' less than stellar years.

The public statements made by the various Chicago area Muslim advocacy and civic engagement groups prompted the chairman of the Cubs organization, Tom Ricketts, son of the person who made the offensive comments, to issue an official apology on behalf of the team. Joe Ricketts himself publicly apologized and expressed regret for his remarks, saying, "I strongly believe that bigoted ideas are wrong." (Sweeney, 2019)

Chicago's Muslim advocacy organizations accepted the apologies offered by Joe Ricketts, even though Ricketts himself was no longer involved in the operations of the franchise, as well as the apology by the Cubs. As a gesture of good will, the Cubs invited a member of the Chicago area Muslim community to throw the ceremonial first pitch at a baseball game at the team's hallowed, historic Wrigley Field. On July 15, 2019, local Palestinian American activist, community organizer and founder of the Inner City Muslim Action Network (IMAN), Rami Nashashibi walked up to the pitcher's mound and threw the baseball toward home plate before a sell-out crowd. (Sweeney, 2019) Such an act is considered an honor in baseball and reserved for people of note or for recognition of something significant. While the event certainly carried meaning for the Chicago Muslim community in that it showed the Cubs' contrition and effort to rectify a wrong that had been committed, Nashashibi nonetheless worried that the gesture would be an unsatisfactory and inadequate closure to the incident, and could serve as an unintended distraction without addressing the persistent challenge of xenophobia and racism and the ease and impunity by which it had and could again be deployed. The Cubs organization and local Muslim organizations continue to engage with each other to combat Islamophobia and bigotry.

It is one thing for random bigots to target Muslim Americans with threatening, anonymous messages of hate and violence, just as the reckless statements of the wealthy and powerful corporate leaders do little to instil a sense of inclusion and belonging. When those who have sworn on oath to protect and serve the public disparage and demonize the very people who rely upon fairness, impartiality and justice from such individuals, public trust suffers a potentially irreversible trauma. In June 2019, a Chicago area police officer was discovered to have posted anti-Muslim messages via his Facebook account. Lieutenant Richard Moravec, a veteran of the Chicago Police Department, was being investigated for allegations of misconduct. Authorities discovered he had been actively posting bigoted messages against Muslims and other groups on Facebook as well as being a member of known hate groups on the site. One such message that Moravec posted read, "Any Islamist insults infidels, I will put him under my feet." He is currently still under investigation for misconduct. (McGhee, 2019)

On occasion, Islamophobia and anti-Muslim bigotry is not just something experienced by the Muslim community itself. After 9-11, for example, several members of the American Sikh community were the victims of violence and hate by those who mistook them for being Muslim. In addition, there is also a danger from Islamophobes to those who show solidarity with the Muslim community and identify themselves as allies. Larycia Hawkins was the first African American woman to receive tenure at Wheaton College, a small Evangelical institution established in 1860, and located about 30 minutes from downtown Chicago. In December 2015, as a response to toxic, anti-Muslim rhetoric from then candidate Donald Trump, Professor Hawkins announced on Facebook that she would be wearing the hijab on campus to show her solidarity with Muslims, especially Muslim women whom the hijab made a visible target for discrimination, bigotry and potential harassment and violence. The college administrators reacted to Professor Hawkins's declaration by placing her on leave and then subsequently terminating her employment, despite her tenured status. They claimed that she acted outside the principles, values and ethos of Wheaton College. Reports indicate that the college faced a strong backlash and criticism from its alumni, some of whom were prolific and significant donors to Wheaton's endowment. They threatened to withhold further donations unless and until the college took action against what they perceived was an unacceptable gesture toward Islam and Muslims.

Professor Hawkins is a committed Christian, and she affirmed that her impetus for wearing the hijab came directly from her Christian values. Hawkins stated that she was trying to replicate Jesus' behavior toward the beleaguered and the vulnerable as a response to Donald Trump's call for a complete and total ban on Muslims seeking entry to the United States. The Muslim community of Chicago as well as the broader Muslim American community showered Professor Hawkins with its appreciation for her solidarity and for the sacrifice she made to her professional career in the name of upholding her Christian values and standing with Muslims. (Graham, 2016)

Arguably the most famous victim of transferred Islamophobia in America, Professor Hawkins is currently within the general faculty in the departments of politics and religious studies at the prestigious and internationally renowned University of Virginia, where she serves as faculty in the Religion, Race, and Democracy Lab. She is also a co-convener of the Religion and Its Publics Project of the Henry Luce Foundation, and is a faculty fellow on the Race, Faith, and Culture Project at the University's Institute for Advanced Studies in Culture.

Detroit

Detroit, Michigan is known as the Motor City. For over a century, it has been home to America's and, arguably, the world's automobile industry. It is the city where Henry Ford pioneered the use of the assembly line and mass production for his car company, inspiring others to capitalize on the local synergy to develop and open their own automobile corporations, like Chrysler and General Motors. Detroit has been synonymous with manufacturing and the working-class ethos of America's heartland and the Midwest. A key port city in the middle of the Great Lakes basin, Detroit benefited from the relative proximity to an abundant supply of iron ore that served as the basic ingredient for industrial output. At its apogee in the 1950s, Detroit had a population of, and infrastructure built for, 2.5 million people. Unfortunately, as the nation's manufacturing base started to erode, shifting to other areas, such as the south and west, as well as with the emergence of competition from other countries, Detroit's economy began to fray, creating significant social strain, including racial tension. These pressures finally came to a head in 1967, with the infamous Detroit riots, which saw African Americans being securitized and white Detroiters leaving the city for the suburbs. As a result, Detroit became, and remains, one of America's most racially segregated and divided metropolitan areas. The so-called "White Flight" of the 1960s and 1970s decimated Detroit's tax base and financial buoyancy. Coupled with devasting economic recessions in the early 1980s and early

21st century, Detroit has struggled to restore its former splendor and stability. Crime and political corruption have not helped the city gain sufficient balance for recovery, and in 2013, Detroit became the largest municipality in the United States to declare bankruptcy. While it emerged stronger from bankruptcy protection, the process to regrow the economy remains a challenge. Efforts are underway to diversify the automobile dominated revenue base, and to entice people to move to the area with new and innovative career opportunities combined with the relatively low cost of living. With a current population of approximately 673,000, a mere shadow of its former status as America's fourth largest city, Detroit continues to be a destination for new arrivals, especially immigrants from around the world, and especially from the so-called Muslim world. The first mosque was built in 1921, in the Detroit enclave of Highland Park, by Mohammad Karoub, a Lebanese businessman. He was one of a multitude of Muslim arrivals from the Levant, drawn to Detroit by Henry Ford's invitation to work in his automobile company's assembly lines. This "pull" factor quickly made Detroit a destination for Middle Easterners of several different religions and denominations, leading to Detroit having the highest concentration of Arabs outside the Middle East. Not all Arabs worked for the car companies; many were entrepreneurial and set up small businesses like grocery stores, restaurants and service-based entities. In 1921, the Muslim population of Detroit was estimated at 16,000. (Howell, 2014)

Not all of Detroit's Muslims in the 1920s and 1930s were Arab; Muslims from the former Ottoman Empire migrated from Albania and Bosnia, while others arrived from North Africa. In addition, the African American Muslim community had its origins in Detroit with the establishment of the Nation of Islam, by W.D. Fard in the early 1930s, when he founded Temple #1 in the city. Today, Detroit is home to large Muslim communities from Albania, Bosnia, Iraq, Lebanon, Syria, Palestine, Egypt, India, Pakistan, Bangladesh, Somalia, West Africa (Nigeria, Senegal, Gambia), as well as a sizable African American Muslim community. (Howell, 2014) The estimated Muslim population of metropolitan Detroit is 200,000 out of a total population of 2.5 million for the region. There are an estimated 70 mosques and Islamic centers, representing all denominations within Islam.

There are also approximately ten full-time Islamic schools in the area. (www.cairmichigan.org)

Muslims from Detroit serve in the United States Congress. Since her election in 2018, Rashida Tlaib has represented Michigan's 13 Congressional district, which includes most of Southwest Detroit and the Arab concentrated city of Dearborn. Abdullah Hammoud represents Dearborn as a Representative in Michigan's State Legislature located in the state capital, Lansing. In 2018, Abdul El-Sayed, a young Egyptian-American, made an unsuccessful bid to become the first Muslim governor in America, losing in the primaries to eventual victor, Gretchen Whitmer. Muslims also serve as judges and hold several positions in local government. (Warikoo, 2019)

The Detroit enclave of Hamtramck, once the home to the nation's largest Polish immigrant population, now has a vibrant, multi-ethnic community of 30,000 people, including large numbers of Muslims from the Balkans, Yemen, as well as the largest concentration of Bangladeshis in the country. In 2015, Hamtramck became the first city in the nation to have a majority Muslim city council. It affirms both the electability of Muslim candidates within an American polity and also demonstrates the acknowledgement by Muslim immigrants of the importance of civil and political engagement, not just at the national level but within their own respective locales, confirming the adage that all politics is indeed local.

Hamtramck's Muslim community has not been immune to controversy, especially criticisms that approach xenophobia and bigotry based upon religious and ethnic categories. In 2004, a mosque in the city started to broadcast the call to prayer (*adhaan*) over loudspeakers. Some residents complained that the sound violated the city's noise ordinance and disturbed the peace. They also criticized the timing of the adhaan, including its broadcast in the early morning (fajr) hours, sometimes before 6am, and late at night (11pm). Muslim community leaders reminded the critics that church bells pealed freely during times of service and had continued without complaint from any of Hamtramck's residents for years. Eventually, the city and the Muslim community agreed upon a resolution whereby the *adhaan* could continue be broadcast outdoors but within certain time allowances and at a set volume to minimize any inconvenience, while still being in compliance with noise regulations for the city. (Aghajanian, 2017)

Of course, Islamophobes, both in the media and throughout civil society, wasted no time in condemning the city and the community for reaching an agreement that allowed the adhaan to be broadcast. The bigots accused Hamtramck of yielding to the onslaught and imposition of sharia law and warned that the decision was a harbinger of things to come in other cities across the United States. Fortunately, such malicious and mendacious hysteria failed to gain any significant traction in the American population at large.

The high visibility in the public imagination of Dearborn as a center of Arab and Muslim American life has made it a frequent and convenient target for Islamophobes throughout the United States. Notwithstanding such defamatory aspersions as branding the city as a "no-go zone" for non-Muslims, as well as being a city where sharia law governs the entire population, Muslim and non-Muslim alike, racists and xenophobes have turned Dearborn into a totem of their hatred of Muslims. It is irrelevant to them that not all Muslims are Arabs and that all Arabs are not Muslim; after all, Detroit is home to a very large Arab Christian population, mostly from Lebanon, Iraq, Palestine and Syria. Islamophobes seeking to score political or social points with their brethren threaten to travel to Dearborn to agitate and provoke some kind of reaction from the city's residents that could then prove their assertion that Muslims are hostile and willing to commit violence against "Americans."

In 2009, a group of self-professed Christian missionaries descended upon Dearborn during the city's annual Arab International Festival, a three-day gathering that celebrates Arab culture with food, entertainment and shopping. The festival is not Muslim, given the diverse, multi-religious nature of the Arab community and all are welcome to attend and participate in the various programs and events. The missionaries made their way into the festival area and started to berate Arab attendees, shouting that "they were going to hell because they were Muslim." It was immaterial to the Christian zealots that they were yelling their invectives at a crowd that included several children who were shocked and frightened by the spectacle, or that many of the Arabs to whom they were directing their religious pronouncements were in fact Christians themselves. For these

Christian agitators, an Arab Christian was essentially a Muslim as he/she was perceived and prejudged primarily by their race rather than their belief system. (Warikoo, 2013)

The Dearborn Arab International Festival is a frequent target of racists and Islamophobes. In 2012, a Christian group known as the Bible Believers converged on the festival with pig's head that they had mounted on a pole, and carried signs denigrating, in extremely vile and profane terms, Islam as well as the Prophet Mohammed. The provocateurs claimed that they had every right to assemble in a public space and exercise their First Amendment right to free speech, no matter how offensive and insulting it may be. Although they were arrested for disturbing the peace, the Bible Believers defeated the subsequent prosecution by using the defense of free speech. The Arab-American Chamber of Commerce then made the decision, in coordination with the city of Dearborn, to move the festival away from public spaces. (Warikoo, 2013)

Dearborn's position as the recipient of Islamophobic attention often occurs when events involving Muslims present themselves elsewhere in the United States. In the summer of 2010, New York City became the focus of considerable controversy over the planned construction of the so-called "Ground Zero Mosque" (Park 51 Center) in lower Manhattan. The decision by a group of Muslim Americans to build a Muslim cultural center that also had a prayer space was seized by Islamophobes to unleash a campaign of hate not only at the developers but also against Muslims across the country. Claiming that the site of the 9-11 World Trade Center attacks, Ground Zero, was somehow, "hallowed ground," opponents of the project took to the media airwaves to condemn the plans as insensitive at best and more maliciously, impugning Muslims collectively and accusing them of imposing their will despite having been implicitly responsible for the destruction of the buildings in the first place and causing the deaths of 3,000 innocent people. In actuality, the proposed Park 51 center was several blocks away from Ground Zero, a neighborhood that was home to bars, restaurants, stores and even a strip club, none of which apparently desecrated the sanctity and sacrality of the site. Eventually, the development project fell through and the center was not constructed, but the fervor and venom directed at the Muslim American community was palpable and felt throughout the country. It even inspired and emboldened other Islamophobes to capitalize on the issue and advance their own agendas; some were even purportedly men of God.

The Reverend Terry Jones is pastor at the Dove World Outreach Center in Gainesville, Florida, home to the University of Florida, and two hours north of Orlando. He is also author of the book, *Islam is the Devil* and president of the group, Stand Up America Now, a political organization whose mission is to oppose radical Islam and the moral decline of America. Of course, to Jones and his acolytes, the only type of Islam is radical Islam as Jones believes the faith is inherently violent and its followers seek to impose sharia law throughout the country and the world.

In July 2010, commensurate with the ongoing "Ground Zero Mosque" controversy, Reverend Jones announced that he planned to burn 200 copies of the Qur'an to mark the 9th anniversary of the September 11 attacks. He received worldwide attention and considerable condemnation for his threat, while at the same time being hailed a hero by many Islamophobes. His proclamation evoked protests and demonstrations in many Muslim societies in the world, including in Afghanistan, leading to several deaths and injuries there. Jones eventually decided against holding the event and in fact declared that he would never burn a Qur'an. His pledge was short-lived and empty. In March 2011, Jones placed the Qur'an "on trial" for its alleged violence and anti-American values. He then proceeded to "convict and sentence" the Qur'an by burning a copy in his Gainesville church. The following month, Jones planned to travel to Dearborn and stage a provocative protest in front of the Islamic Center of America, the largest mosque in the country, and a highly prominent center due to its distinctive and grand architecture and aesthetics. (Hafiz, 2014) Jones was confronted by a "peace chain" of hundreds of Muslims and people of other faiths who came to reject Jones's message of hate.

Reverend Jones' is not the only American religious leader to traffic in Islamophobia. More recently, the Bloomfield Hills Baptist Church, representing an affluent suburb north of Detroit, published a flyer promoting a "discussion" titled, "An Eye on Islamism," featuring self-professed "Proud Islamophobe," Pastor Dr. Donald McKay. The event was sponsored and organized by the Metropolitan Detroit Freedom Coalition, which, despite its inclusive and benign sounding moniker, is a right-wing organization that has been accused of holding racist and Islamophobic views. The event was scheduled to occur on September 11th and 12th, intentionally to coincide with the 9-11 anniversary.

Pastor McKay has been on record, saying, "I am an Islamophobe, I wear that badge proudly." He has also contended, "We believe that Muslims, committed Muslims, that are familiar with their faith are committed really to the overthrown of the United States and to world domination." He tried to blunt accusations of Islamophobia and bigotry by arguing, "We don't hate Muslims, we hate the ideology they are identified with."

As news of the "Eye on Islamism" seminar spread, local lawmakers as well as other religious and community leaders condemned the event and also condemned the church for agreeing to host it, arguing that such rhetoric was divisive, unproductive and un-Christian. Facing such blistering criticism, the Bloomfield Baptist Church relented and decided to cancel the program. (Kuruvilla, 2014)

The volatile conditions of the Middle East and other parts of the so-called Muslim world inevitably keep Muslim Americans on the radar of both civil society as well as government agencies that consider the community to be a security threat. The diverse, sizable and easily identifiable Muslim community of the metropolitan Detroit area makes it a constant focus of attention. While it is a community that has learned to cope with the unreasonable public glare of suspicion and xenophobia, some of the scrutiny, especially from the security authorities, is based upon particulars such as country of national or ethnic origin or by denomination. A significant part of Dearborn's population is Lebanese Shi'i, specifically from southern Lebanon, including many from the village of Bint Jebail. The memories and scars of the Lebanese Civil War are still fresh in the minds of many families that live in Dearborn, especially the trauma of the 1982 Israeli invasion of southern Lebanon as well as more recent incursions, such as the 2006 war that damaged not only villages near the border but also a recently rebuilt Beirut. Every summer, hundreds of Lebanese Shi'i from Dearborn travel to Lebanon and spend several months there. They have invested heavily in the local economy, with many maintaining a second home there.

For the United States government, Hizbullah is a designated terrorist organization. The US State Department does not make the distinction, as do several other countries. between Hizbullah's political wing- it is a legitimate and duly elected representative, not to mention influential, part of the Lebanese parliament- or its function as the prime NGO in southern Lebanon, and its paramilitary branch. For the United States, anything associated with Hizbullah is a terrorist enterprise. This creates a rather paradoxical situation for the US government, which recognizes the Lebanese government as being the legitimate sovereign representative of the country, despite its inclusion of Hizbullah. The United States has not imposed any sanctions on the government or the country. In fact, one could make the reasonable argument that by engaging at any level with the Lebanese government, the United States is officially violating its own designation by lending material support to a terrorist entity. Of course, the United States government will not accept such violations from its citizenry, even if it is not troubled by the contradictory, perhaps hypocritical activity in which it engages itself. For the Dearborn Lebanese Shi'i community, the possibility of being charged with such a crime always looms over it. It does not deter the community from being open, active and even vocal supporters and sympathizers of Hizbullah. It is an open question as to whether or how the community might demonstrate its support for Hizbullah without running afoul of existing US laws that prohibit lending material support to it. After all, Hizbullah does operate as a well-recognized and well-respected charity in southern Lebanon, providing basic humanitarian services to the community, both in times of war and peace. Clearly, explicit donations to Hizbullah affiliated organizations would be problematic vis-à-vis American law, and it is a well-accepted presumption that the US government carefully monitors any and all financial transactions between the Dearborn community and individuals or institutions in Lebanon. Given Hizbullah's close ties to the Iranian government and with current American foreign policy toward Iran being particularly toxic and bellicose, it is unclear whether Dearborn will continue to face the specter of increased suspicion and surveillance or whether even more drastic action may be taken. The Trump Administration has issued the United States Customs and Border Protection Agency a directive to detain all Iranians, irrespective of citizenship status, as they are entering or leaving the country for additional screening and interrogation. This development demonstrates that even possession of a US passport provides no immunity from being profiled and treated as a suspected enemy of the state.

Likewise, other subgroups of Detroit's Muslim community have been targeted and profiled based upon conflagrations overseas. At various times in the past 10 years, Yemeni Americans, Somali Americans and any Muslims traveling near or to Syria have faced increased scrutiny at the airport and suspected enhanced surveillance in and around Detroit. They have been painted by a broad brush as being potential extremists traveling to and from ISIS training camps or having engaged in actual combat. To date, no Detroit area Muslim American has been proven to have been a member of a terrorist enterprise, whether Al Qaeda, ISIS, Al Shabab or other terrorist designated entities. (Kundnani, 2014)

Government officials have also been accused of "manufacturing" terrorists in the absence of actual terrorists in the Dearborn area. In February 2016, Khalil Abu Rayyan, a 22-year-old Palestinian American Muslim was arrested on charges of suspected terrorism links because of statements of sympathy and support for ISIS that he made to an undercover FBI agent over the telephone. Rayyan was allegedly recorded boasting how he planned to shoot people at a local Detroit church and that he also planned to kill a Detroit police officer. It emerged through the legal proceedings that Rayyan suffered from mental health problems and the undercover agent to whom he was speaking was allegedly flirting with him to entice him into making incriminating statements. Rayyan is said to have been trying to impress his supposed paramour with bravado and by pretending to be connected to dangerous activities. The federal prosecutors were unsuccessful in pushing the terrorism indictments and Rayyan eventually pled guilty to gun charges, including making a false statement to acquire a firearm. He was sentenced to five years in prison without anything tying him to the original terrorism accusation. (Warikoo. 2017)

The Metro Detroit region is home to a sizable and visible

Muslim community and not all its members hail from immigrant backgrounds. The African American Muslim community, one of the city's oldest Muslim groups, has also not been immune to the toxicity of Islamophobia and securitization. In October 2009, dozens of FBI agents and local law enforcement officers raided a Detroit warehouse. The authorities were seeking to execute an arrest warrant based on information of possible fencing of stolen merchandise. The target of the arrest warrant was Imam Luqman Ameen Abdullah, a 53-year-old African American religious leader who was well known, liked and respected in the local community. (Kundnani, 2014) He was responsible for running soup kitchens and providing housing for the poor through resources from his mosque on the city's west side.

While details of the raid are vigorously disputed by both the Muslim community of Detroit and federal authorities alike, what is known is that Imam Abdullah was killed in a hail of gunfire. His autopsy reveals that he was shot more than 20 times and died on the scene. FBI agents claim that Abdullah was armed and refused to surrender his weapon when authorities demanded he disarm. Abdullah's supporters, however, maintain that the FBI conducted a massive cover up of the incident, concealing exculpatory evidence and in fact planting evidence designed to corroborate their version of events. Such manipulation of the facts would be essential to justify such firepower and results for a criminal matter that allegedly only involved stolen property.

Andrew Arena, the FBI special agent in charge of the investigation went on record to describe Abdullah as "the leader of a domestic terrorist group." Arena conceded that Abdullah was not being pursued at the time on any terrorism charges, but justified his bureau's actions and the ensuing consequences by contending, "where we don't charge a person with terrorism, [we] charge them with whatever we can, to get them off the streets." Information emerged that Abdullah was deprived of medical attention even though the FBI's dog, wounded in the raid, was immediately airlifted to a hospital for treatment to wounds it had suffered during the melee. After the fact, the FBI tried to frame the narrative about Imam Abdullah to justify their actions by attesting in their criminal affidavit that Abdullah was in fact the leader of a "radical, fundamentalist" African-American Muslim group, whose goal was to impose sharia law both locally and across the country. No evidence has ever been presented to corroborate such a contention and the Metro Detroit community strongly refuted the accusations and attempts to disparage a murdered man. (Kundnani, 2014) The FBI also contended that their investigation was part of a four-year long effort that involved multiple informants that had infiltrated Imam Abdullah's community to accumulate the necessary evidence required to obtain the arrest warrant in question. If false, then it would indicate yet another ploy to obfuscate the true impetus and circumstances around the issue. If, on the other hand, such disclosure is true, then it is a stunning and bold admission of what has long been suspected by the Detroit Muslim community of the depth and scope of government surveillance and securitization.

Abdullah's affiliations with other Muslim and African activists appear to have played a role in the federal authorities' treatment and excessive use of force to neutralize him. Abdullah was friends with former Black Panther leader and Muslim activist H. Rap Brown, also known as Jamil Al-Amin, himself serving a prison sentence on charges of murdering a police officer in 2002, under circumstances that bring into question the certitude of his guilt. For the African American community, the reality of "guilt by association" has been a constant element of their interaction with law enforcement officials and the government, both at local and national levels. It has been the target and subject of the federal COINTELPRO policy of the FBI and various affiliates for at least 60 years. It is a policy that has been extended to other suspect groups since, including Muslim Americans. (Kundnani, 2014)

The history of the Detroit Muslim community, along with its diversity, size and relationship to the complex and volatile geopolitics involving the so-called Muslim world and US government has made it well acclimated and equipped to cope with, even expect, continued securitization and surveillance by law enforcement agencies and authorities. While it is an unpleasant reality, the community's resilience is based on its pragmatic stance of understanding the capabilities and contradictions of government rhetoric and policies toward itself and other suspect groups.

Chapter 4

A Theoretical Approach to Hatred in the USA

Compared to other western countries, hate crimes have a longer history in the United States. The term "hate crime" first appeared in the USA in the late 1980s as a way to determine the severity of racialized hatred in the Howard Beach area of New York City, in which a black man was killed while trying to escape from the hands of a gang of white teenagers (Naidoo, 2016).

Hate crimes against individuals and groups include a wide range of criminal behaviors, including discrimination, intimidation, harassment, sabotage, assault, and murder, which vary in their severity and impact on society. These types of crimes have a common foundation in hatred. Moreover, the tendency to violence in these types of crimes is greater than in other crimes.

Hate crimes are also known by other terms. The most common of these terms is "bias crime", which emphasizes that such offenses often result from prejudice against an individual or group of people. In the 1990s, Howard Ehrlich (1990), director of the Institute of Arbitration at Towson State University, coined the term "ethno-violence" to include cases that did not meet the legal standard of a crime but contained an element of prejudice. This is why, as incorporated in the concept of hate crime, the use of the term "hate" implies terms such as "bigotry", "bias", "prejudice", "ethno-violence" and "ethnocentrism".

Over the past few decades, the number of hate crimes has risen by alarming proportions. As criminologists Jack Levin and Jack McDevitt (1993) pointed out in the 1990s, "hate crimes have become a growing threat to the well-being of our society – on the college campus, in the workplace, and around our neighborhoods" (Levin and McDevitt, 1993).

In response to national concerns about crimes of bigotry, the US Congress passed the Hate Crime Statistics Act of 1990, which ordered the Attorney General to collect data on hate crimes. Also, The Church Arson Act of 1996 stipulated that data collection of hate crimes should become a permanent part of the Uniform Crime Reporting (UCR) Program. Hate crime refers to "criminal acts which are seen to have been motivated by bias against one or more persons or social groups, or by bias against their derivatives. Incidents may involve physical assault, damage to property, bullying, harassment, verbal abuse or insults, hate crime or offensive graffiti or letters" (Streissguth, 2003: 3).

Racialized Islamophobia

Hate crimes against Muslims in the United States can be explained by the concept of racialization. In general terms, racism if often understood to depend on the physical characteristics of the victim's choice (Dunn et al., 2007). However in Western societies, the two central elements of Orientalism and Islamophobia have led to racism against Muslims and the social construction of a "visible archetype" (Meer and Modood, 2009) of Muslims, which is incompatible with "Western" culture and religion. Racism against Muslims in the United States represents both an ideological and historical process that expands the meaning of race in Islamic communities and Muslims (Omi and Winant, 1994). The structures of Orientalism and Islamophobia are assumed to be characterized by instability, inferiority, and incompatibility; the main components that are the main tools of racism in the United States. American Muslims are embroiled in a "clash of racializations" between the deprivation of American national identity and racialized Muslimness (Carr and Haynes, 2015), both of which expose Muslims to racist activities and at the same time deprive them of government support.

Despite the ethnic heterogeneity of the American Muslim population, Muslims in the United States are defined by 'race'. This means that they are identified as a potential threat based on racial characteristics. This racial identity is the process by which Muslims are identified and labeled through racial differences, such as skin color, as well as through culturally understood characteristics of Islamic symbols, such as beards or headscarves. The same institutionalized racism, in the discourse of the "war on terror," is considered "in the dichotomy between the benevolent, the deviant masculinity of the 'brown man'" (Khalid, 2011: 20). This gendered Orientalist representation relies on multiple dichotomies, but also uses a racist hierarchy (ibid.). Islamophobia supports demonizing Muslims as threats that need to be managed through racial classification, coercion, and violence.

The UK Runnymede Trust's (1997) report, Islamophobia: A Challenge for Us All, so far, has spawned many studies based on its findings. This institution considered Islamophobia as a specific mechanism by which Islam is defined as a monolithic bloc, static and unresponsive to change, a separated Other without values in common with other cultures, inferior to the West, barbaric, irrational, primitive, sexist, violent, aggressive, threatening, supportive of terrorism, engaged in a clash of civilizations, a political ideology.

The relationship between Islamophobia and racism shows that race is more related to social structure than to biology. Race is a social and historical concept, expressing specific social relations in a historical context (Omi and Winant, 1994). The 17th century conception of race determined by physical differences is currently not accepted by most sociologists, anthropologists, and biologists. Race science now focuses solely on the social reproduction of race, which is why the American Scientist (2011) refers to race as "folk taxonomy, not science." While geographically, there are differences in human biology, such as differences in the treatment of certain diseases, these differences are not significantly related to race. By emphasis on the difference between the two propositions, "there is no such thing as race" and "there is no biological entity that warrants the term 'race',", Brace (2000) shows how a superstitious and intentional belief puts itself in the place of science.

Various polls show that the behavior of the non-Muslim majority in the United States has become more hostile to Muslims. This situation has paralleled the intensification of hatred in the discourse of politicians and in the representation of the media. The latest collection of data on Islamophobic hate crimes by the Council on American-Islamic Relations (CAIR) (2017) shows that between 2014 and 2016, anti-Muslim hate crimes increased by 65 percent. In 2016 alone, Islamophobia increased by 57 percent. CAIR's findings are similar to those collected by the Center for the Study of Hate and Extremism (CSHE) at California State University San Bernardino, which recorded 196 hate crimes in 2015 in 20 states; 29 percent more than the 154 cases in 2014 for the whole country (Levin, 2016). In 2010 anti-Muslim hate crimes increased from 107 to 160 cases (49.5 percent) (Levin, 2016). The "Ground Zero Mosque" controversy in New York (Levin 2016) occurred during the same period. Also, attacks on Muslims as a percentage of the total hate crimes increased in this period (Lichtblau, 2016).

Of all the religious groups in the United States, Muslims face the most prejudice (Pew Research Center, 2014). In 2015, negative attitudes toward American Muslims increased to 67 percent (Arab American Institute, 2015). A Huffington Post poll of Americans' views on Muslims found that 55 percent of respondents had a "quantitative or very unfavorable view" of Islam, while one in four said they were unsure of the meaning of Islamic faith (Kaleem, 2015). Of the Americans polled by the Huffington Post, only 10 percent said they had ever been to a mosque, and 44 percent said they did not want to know more about Islam. In addition to their completely unfavorable views on Islam, a large percentage (42 percent) of Americans believe that law enforcement agencies are right to use racial tactics against Muslims and Arabs (Siddiqui, 2014). These trends play a central role in Islamophobic sentiments. In addition, Zogby Analytics, a legal advocacy group, found that support for Muslims living in the United States in 2014 was only 27 percent, compared to 36 percent in 2010 (Siddiqui, 2014). Studies have also shown that anti-Islamic sentiment is more common among Americans over the age of 45, Republicans, and whites (Chalabi, 2015).

By classifying a variety of hate crimes against Muslims in the United States into three different categories, Ameli, Mohseni Ahooei, and Merali (2013) found that 32.1 percent of Muslims in the United States experienced interpersonal Islamophobia in their everyday life. The figure for Ideological Islamophobia, which means experiencing hate because of belief or faith, was 25.7 percent and for the experience of Islamophobic policy it was 44.9 percent. The experience of hate crimes among Muslims in the United States is second only to the UK and greater than France and Canada.

A key point about the spread of hate crimes against Muslims is that such crimes are not limited to Muslims. This fact proves the existence of racialized Islamophobia in the United States. In May 2016, an Italian economist, Guido Menzio, was thrown off a US airliner after being seen writing mathematical equations on a notebook. Menzio was described by a passenger as someone with "dark, curly hair, with an exotic foreign accent." He was ejected from the plane and taken for questioning (Danner, 2016). Authorities told him he was suspected of terrorism. The Menzio case is an illustration of the way prejudice against Islam and Muslims in the United States works.

Based on such evidence, Chu (2015) argues that the philosophy of Islamophobia is not the result of "intellectual disagreement" with the principles of Islam, but rather the result of historical xenophobic distrust in America towards all those who are different from 'ordinary' Americans. When Islamophobic hate crimes engulfed the American Sikh community after 9-11, Chu's theory was substantiated. Sikh communities across the United States are victims of hate crimes by Americans. Post-9-11 incidents and concerns over rising hate crimes have led to the formation of the Sikh Coalition, now the largest Sikh civil rights organization in the United States (Basu, 2016). In the first month after 9-11, the Coalition documented more than 300 cases of violence and discrimination against Sikhs in the United States (Basu, 2016). Fifteen years after 9-11, many Sikhs continue to feel insecure in America, largely because of the inability of perpetrators of hate crimes to distinguish between Sikhs and Muslims (Basu, 2016).

The data presented on hate crimes against American Muslims and non-Muslims in the United States shows that "Muslim identity" (Samari, 2016: 1921) is racialized. Sikhs and other "Muslim-looking" people continue to experience hate crimes because of their identities (Sikh Coalition, 2015). The Sikh Coalition claims that the formal classification of hate crimes against Sikhs is necessary "because it is not possible to address the problem unless it is accurately measured" (Sikh Coalition, 2012: 3).

The media is a major contributor to the rise of Islamophobia throughout the United States. According to Media Tenor International, a study that investigates the data of NGOs and governments, news media such as Fox, NBC and CBS most emphasized violence in the representation of Islam between 2007 and 2013 (Media Tenor International, 2011). Media Tenor International also found that US and European news media coverage of the Middle East mainly focused on Muslim militancy (Media Tenor International, 2011).

The entertainment industry also aids anti-Islamic racism and exacerbates anti-Islam and anti-Muslim sentiment. In a study of news coverage by LexisNexis Academic and CNN about all terrorist attacks in the United States between 2011 and 2015, researchers found that the media focussed significantly on attacks from Muslims, especially ones born outside the United

States (Kearns et al., 2017a). The number of attacks perpetrated by Muslims represented in these media are on average 449 percent greater than non-Muslim attacks (Kearns et al., 2017b). Erin Kearns, author of the study, told National Public Radio (NPR) in June 2017 that when it comes to a Muslim terrorist attack, "you can expect to receive four and a half times more media coverage than if the perpetrator was not Muslim."

The concept "racial formation," coined by Omi and Winant (1994), is useful for understanding the ways in which media content defines Muslim identities in a way that is intertwined with racial meanings. The reaction of Americans to action movies, and the increasing use of Arabs and Muslims as villains, shows how Americans' perceptions of the Arab and Muslim population can be shaped (Wilkins, 2008). Jack Shaheen, author of *Reel Bad Arabs: How Hollywood Vilifies People* and *A is for Arab: Archiving Stereotypes in U.S. Popular Culture*, has analyzed the way Arabs are portrayed in American movies and television over the past century (Shaheen, 2012). Shaheen shows how Hollywood portrays Arabs as "brute murderers, sleazy rapists, religious fanatics, oil-rich dimwits and abusers of women." Shaheen's research covers more than 1,000 movies depicting Arabs, showing that 932 movies portrayed them using negative stereotypes. Only 12 movies had a positive image. He also shows movies portraying Arabs as slaves or a vicious terrorist seeking to destroy Western civilization. Omi and Winant (1994) suggest that these representations lead to a kind of "racial etiquette" or set of specific racial meanings that act in the daily interactions of people living in the United States, intensifying the stereotypes of the Middle East as a place for extremism and terrorism and Muslims as terrorists. Such representations support policies that have dire consequences for Arabs, Muslims, as well as those who appear to be Muslims (Alsultany, 2015). These manipulated images of Arabs and Muslims gives "permission to hate", which often appears with a combination of racial and religious discrimination (Poynting and Mason, 2006: 367).

In addition to official discourse and media representation, Islamophobia in the United States is also exacerbated by the "Islamophobia industry" (Lean, 2012). In recent years, anti-Muslim groups and organizations have benefited from at least $205 million to spread fear and hatred against Muslims (Council on American-Islamic Relations, 2016: V). In 2011, the Center for American Progress (CAP), a public policy research organization in Washington DC, found that seven charities between 2001 and 2009 donated $ 42.6 million to support expansion of anti-Islamic attitudes in the United States (Ali, 2011). The CAP's report identified several key sources of funding for Islamophobia: the Donors Capital Fund, the Richard Mellon Scaife Foundation, the Lynde and Harry Bradley Foundation, the Newton and Rochelle Becker Foundation and Newton and Rochelle Becker Charitable Trust, the Russell Berrie Foundation, the Anchorage Charitable Fund and William Rosenwald Family Fund, and the Fairbrook Foundation (Ali, 2011).

Divided States of America

In the United States, the history of crimes against humanity, on the one hand, and the history of human rights struggles, on the other, has always revolved around racial issues. The concept of race is still the richest historical myth and the most central concept for shaping the cultural policy that exists in the country. The United States enacted the most shameful racial segregation laws in 1849, when the Massachusetts Supreme Court ruled that schools should operate on the basis of racial segregation under the Constitution of Massachusetts (BlackPast, 2010). Despite increasing racial diversity and the repeal of this law in 1954, the dominance of this over American society remains as cultural policy.

A Washington Post analysis (Williams and Emamdjomeh, 2018) shows that populations in the United States are deeply segregated due to racial diversity. Based on census data from 1990, 2000, 2010 and the latest estimates from a five-year study of the American community in 2016, the analysis maps the habitats of six ethnic groups: black, white, Hispanic, Asian / Pacific Islander, Native American and multiracial / other.

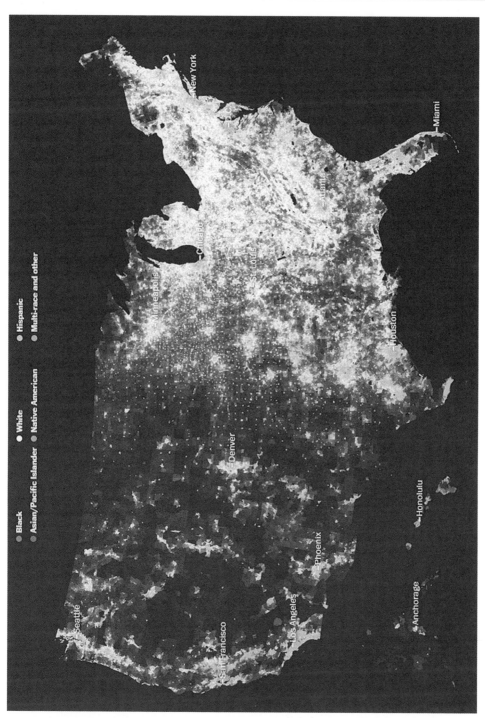

Habitancy map of different races in the United States (Williams and Emamdjomeh, 2018)

While whites live mainly in the northern half of the United States, blacks are mainly concentrated in the southeast and Hispanics and Asian / Pacific Islanders live in the southern and southwestern parts of the country. This map is consistent with the US housing inflation map. In other words, white sectors experience higher price growth in housing (Mellnik et.al. 2016).

Another symbol of the preservation of segregation is the racial composition of schools in the United States. Although a law on the prevention of school separation was passed in 1954, research shows that racial segregation in US schools is greater now than in previous decades (Frankenberg, 2019).

Percentage of students who attend a school with students from predominantly their own ethnicity. (Frankenberg, 2019)

Currently, more than 40 percent of black and Latino students attend segregated schools where at least 9 out of every 10 students are children of color. The majority of students in these schools are from low-income families, and a 2016 government report concluded that students' academic opportunities were damaged. The percentage of black and Latin students in segregated schools has been steadily rising since the late 1980s (Frankenberg, 2019).

In education, the gap between black and white success has largely widened, as the poorest students are concentrated in ethnically homogeneous schools where education is affected by children's out-of-school challenges. These schools are segregated because their neighborhoods are segregated. The growth of inequality to some extent reflects the gap in racial wealth. Middle-class white Americans are more likely to live in neighborhoods with higher house values, while their middle-class counterparts are likely to rent, or live in neighborhoods with stagnant values (Frankenberg, 2019).

For Muslims, this segregation has taken on an intensified form, especially after 9-11. Louis Cainkar (2009) shows the long-term effects of 9-11 on the Muslim communities in the United States. Aiming to demonstrate the day-to-day experiences of Muslims in Chicago, Cainkar describes his experiences of "de-Americanization" in a broader historical context than Islamophobia. His book shows that Arabs and Muslims were angry at the racial prejudice they faced in the years following the 9-11 attacks. Cainkar's study found that respondents felt fear and insecurity in everyday spaces. They also cited a high level of discriminatory experiences. These narratives reveal the negative effects of efficiency, surveillance, ethnic profiling events, and the rules governing the daily lives of American citizens' with Muslim ancestry. Muslims in America are vulnerable to these negative effects. Muslim women in hijab, for example, are more exposed to harm, discrimination and attacks in everyday spaces. Most importantly, after the 9-11 attacks, the governing bodies turned discrimination and hatred policies into the norm against Muslim populations. The de-Americanization process, as Gallup (n.d.) points out, has exacerbated the experience of social non-belonging at the four levels of policy, political discourse, media representation, and everyday experience.

The findings are consistent with the results of hate crimes studies in the United States conducted by the Islamic Human Rights Commission (IHRC), which show the high level of hate crimes of various types regarding interpersonal and ideological Islamophobia and Islamophobic policy (Ameli et al, 2013). The study is based on the Domination Hate Model of Intercultural Relations (DHMIR), which examines hate crimes within the context of an environment of hate which is fueled by hate policy and hate representation. Hate policy and representation develop the environment of hate by producing schemata which lead in turn to a variety of hate crimes and hateful behavior and policy. These findings are also consistent with other studies of hate crimes in terms of the proportion of different experiences of hate crimes and their variety in the UK (Ameli, et al., 2011; Ameli and Merali, 2015), France (Ameli, et al., 2012) and Canada (Ameli and Merali, 2014).

DHMIR was first developed by Ameli (2010), then applied in various contexts. Historical xenophobia and schemata are reproduced through the mass media, politicians' discourse, and especially the relationship between these two main bases. They use cultural signifiers in favor of the central forces in power and against marginalized oppressed minorities to reproduce and empower dichotomy stigmatized patterns (including the most important ones, Us and Others). The stigmatized individuals and groups as Others are considered a threat, and thus their suppression becomes natural and legitimized. The normalization of repression extends the hate crimes to the point of naturalization. These all amount to a domination policy (Ameli, 2010).

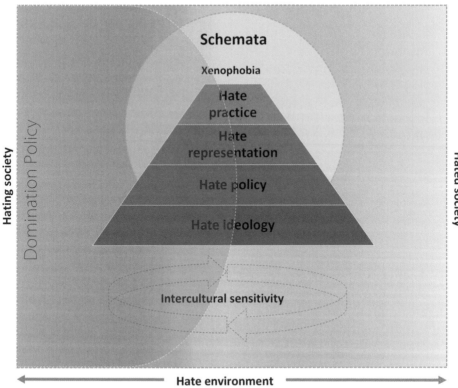

Domination Hate Model of Intercultural Relations (DHMIR)

Like any other western country with a Muslim minority, media and policies play a central role in creating a climate of hatred in the United States. However, the United States has another third and unique source for developing an environment of hate, which Lean (2012) calls the "Islamophobia industry." The Islamophobia industry's turnover reflects long-term planning and extensive institutions, especially for the development of hatred and Islamophobia. Under the influence of these three sources of hate, four different types of hatred can be distinguished in terms of representation, policy, ideology, and everyday experience (or hate practice).

According to a poll conducted by Telhami (2015), Americans distinguish between the terms Islam and Muslims. They see Islam as more undesirable than Muslims. There may be a number of reasons for this, but in principle, it is probably easier for Americans to express an aversion to an abstract idea (Islam) than for people (Muslims) (Telehami, 2015). That is why hate ideology is more developed based on the activities of the Islamophobia industry in the United States than in other countries.

As we have already stated above, Chu (2015) argues that the philosophy of Islamophobia in the USA is not the result of intellectual disagreement with the principles of Islam, but rather the result of historical xenophobic distrust in America towards all those who are different from 'ordinary' Americans. Therefore, xenophobia has historically been one of the main sources of hate crimes against Muslims in the country. Representation of hate against Muslims in the entertainment media, including in movies, can be explained by the concept of xenophobia.

Despite claims that the United States has entered a "post-racial era," the rules of racial profiling applied to Muslims and Islamic communities after 9-11 are discriminatory and based on racial segregation that occurs everyday in various cities across the country (American Civil Liberties Union, n.d.).

Chapter 5

Data analysis of Muslim Experiences of Hatred, Hostility and Discrimination

The survey of Muslim Experiences of Hatred, Hostility and Discrimination was carried out with 375 participants. Using the simple random sampling method in this study, data was collected through two types of printed and online questionnaires. After collecting the questionnaires and checking the records, it emerged that there were 41 incomplete questionnaires, so all of them were deleted leaving the analysis to be conducted on a sample of 334 records.

In terms of age composition, the highest participation rate is between the ages of 19 and 29, comprising 46.2 percent of participants. In addition, 15.7 percent are over 49 years old and 14.8 percent of them are between the ages of 40 and 49. In terms of gender, 50.3 percent of the participants are male and 49.7 percent female.

In terms of the country of birth, persons from 41 different countries have participated in this survey, of which 47.2 percent are US-born. After the US, India (11.1 percent) and Pakistan (6.6 percent) are the most represented followed by Somalia with 3.9 percent, Saudi Arabia comes in at 2.7 percent and Egypt and 2.1 percent. The remaining 26.4 percent are born in 35 other countries with relatively similar dispersions.

In the case of country of citizenship, 75.5 percent of the participants have declared themselves as US citizens. After this dominant ratio, India (2.7 percent) and Pakistan (1.5 percent) have the largest share of citizenship among the participants. Another thing about this variable is that 6.3 percent of the participants have dual citizenship and 0.9 have triple citizenship. In addition, 2.7 percent left the question unanswered.

In terms of the country of residence, 94.9 percent are US residents, and the remainder have a relatively similar dispersion belonging to four other countries (Australia, India, Pakistan, and Saudi Arabia). 3.3 percent did not answer this question. The individuals who participated in this survey come from different cities and regions.

With regard to ethnic origin, since the purpose of the study is to identify the participants' subjectivity with regard to their ethnic belonging, this question has been designed as an open question. The responses are very broad. Pakistanis (8.7 percent), India (7.5 percent), Palestinians (6.9 percent), Asians (6.3 percent), and Arabs (5.7 percent) respectively are the highest proportions. 3.9 percent of the participants classified themselves as African American, and only 2.4 percent of the participants see themselves as Black. Only 1.8 percent described themselves as White. In addition, 6.3 percent have a combined ethnicity of two or more ethnicities.

In terms of marital status, the largest proportion of respondents are single (52.3 percent) followed by married (43.5 percent), divorced (2.7 percent), and widows (1.5 percent).

In terms of visibly Muslim, most of the participants (54.8 percent) expressed they have an Islamic appearance, and 12.2 percent stated that they were recognized as Muslim for some reason. In contrast, 30.1 percent said they did not have an Islamic appearance. In addition, 2.6 percent said that they were not Muslim but are mistaken by others as Muslims.

A large proportion of contributors (71.3 percent) see a minority (less than one third) of Muslims in their neighborhoods; 9.5 percent consider half of their neighbors to be Muslim, and 5.8 percent declared more than two-thirds of their neighbors to be Muslims. 13.5 percent said they were unaware about the Muslim population in their neighborhoods.

In terms of economic income, the middle-income group is the largest group (with 57.1 percent). Subsequently, 29 percent are in the lower income group and 13.9 percent are in the higher income group. In terms of educational level, 28.5 percent had a bachelor's degree and 22.2 percent had a master's degree. In addition, among the participants, the number of people with a diploma or less is 17.8 percent, which is lower than the percentage of people with a higher education degree.

Among the participants, 43.4 percent are employed, 25.1 percent self-employed and 6.6 percent unemployed. The retirement rate in this research is 3.3 percent, and the proportion of students is 21.6 percent. Through the total employed population, 57.4 percent work in the private sector and 42.6 percent in the public sector.

Finally, in terms of religiousness, the highest percentage belongs to the practising Muslims and highly practising Muslims, which account for 64.2 percent and 21 percent, respectively. 4.2 percent described themselves as non-practicing Muslim, 3.9 percent categorized themselves as secular Muslims, and finally 5.5 percent believe they are originally Muslim but not religious.

According to the theoretical and analytical model, the attitude questions of the survey are classified into five categories, including 'hate practice,' 'hate ideology,' 'hate as discrimination,' cultural schema in the meaning of 'hate representation' in media and 'hate policy.'

Hate practice means the citizen's perception of belonging to a hated community that feels its consequences in his or her everyday life. Hate ideology covers all instances of hatred that are Islamophobic, which mainly includes the observation of actions or speech expressed in society or in the media against Muslims. Hate as discrimination is about a specific type of hate, which shows itself as discrimination in social relations or rules. In addition, hate representation is primarily intended to represent hatred through mass media. Muslims are more sensitive to understanding and receiving this particular type of hatred. Finally, hate policy is about policies adopted by government against Muslim populations.

We know that hate crimes differ in quality. It is clear that seeing hate crime against Muslims in a media representation (such as the negative image of Muslims in a movie) has a far less destructive effect than experiencing physical abuse as a hate practice. It is also clear that the negative effects of each of the hate crimes on the victims will vary depending on the context. For example, viewing a Muslim image as a terrorist in a movie while a Muslim audience watches it alone, compared to watching it with a non-Muslim friend or in a movie theater, may put less psychological pressure on the Muslim audience. On the other hand, a negative representation of a Muslim in the news or a documentary has a greater psychological impact on its Muslim audience than its portrayal in a movie or entertainment. It does not end there. The type of hate crime with all the details is also effective in creating a certain level of pressure on the mind and identity of the audience. Representing Muslims as 'sensitive' individuals is less effective than portraying them as 'terrorists.' The type of emphasis, repetition, redundancy and many other factors are involved.

For these reasons, comparing the types of hate crimes with each other in the quantitative analysis presented here should not mean ignoring the qualitative dimensions of each crime. Obviously, hate crimes in the form of physical abuse are expected to be experienced slightly less than hate crimes in the form of media representation or observation in government policies, but it is clear that the extent of the damage is not the same, and of course, such a measurement is simply not possible.

However, it is clear that the severity of hate crimes is not the same in all five types examined here. The data also proves this. Most of the victims' experiences are in hate policy on hatred of Muslims. After that, hate representation is most intense, followed by hate ideology. Hate practice, and especially the feeling of hate as discrimination, is relatively low in the American Muslim communities.

	N	M	SD	Min	Max
Hate policy	309	3.72	0.819	1	5
Hate representation	312	3.50	0.806	1	5
Hate ideology	321	3.41	0.884	1	5
Hate practice	300	2.08	0.838	1	5
Hate as discrimination	309	1.69	0.886	1	5

Descriptive statistics of the different types of hate crime

Classification of hate crimes into five types, regardless of its analytical value to test the theoretical approach in a specific country, can provide a better explanation in terms of pathology and policy making, identify critical areas in any types of crime in a region or country. The figure below shows the severity of each of these categories in a comparative way.

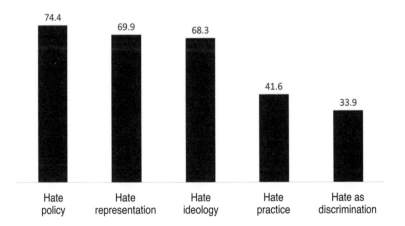

The severity of the experiences based on the types of hate crime

As shown, hate policy with an intensity of 74.4 percent is the most powerful hate experience followed by hate representation in the media and hate ideology. Hate practice regarding citizens' feelings of belonging to a hateful society was far less than the three other categories, and finally, hate as discrimination is the lowest stated experience with 33.9 percent.

Another important issue is the high dispersion (SD: 0.80, 0.88) in this study compared to previous research on hate crimes in the North America and Western Europe[1]. The relatively high level of this indicator reflects a more consistent homogeneity of data and greater diversity in the personal experience of Muslims as victims of hate crimes. It is important to know which type of dispersal is most true about which type of experience. In other words, of which cases of hate crimes do Muslims not have a close view to each other?

---

[1] The extensive evidence of hate crime studies in the USA (Ameli et al., 2013), the UK (Ameli et al., 2011; Ameli and Merali, 2015), Canada (Ameli and Merali, 2014), and France (Ameli, et al., 2012) reflect the correlations between the types of hate crime.

		N	M	SD	Min	Max
Hate policy	Seeing policies or practices at work or school negatively affected Muslim people	316	3.24	1.11	1	5
	Discriminatory acts against Muslims are condoned by politicians	315	3.59	1.07	1	5
	Politicians do not care about Muslims	317	3.67	1	1	5
	Seeing political policies (local or national) that negatively affected Muslim people	317	3.79	1.07	1	5
Hate representation	Those who discriminate against Muslims have an authentic picture about them and their religion	316	2.04	1.38	1	5
	If people know more about Muslims, they would act much better than the way they do now	319	4.19	1.05	1	5
	Those who discriminate against Muslims are highly driven by the media content	317	4.28	0.98	1	5
	Experience of some kind of discrimination but afraid to complain	318	1.39	0.82	1	5
Hate as discrimination	Experience of educational discrimination based on religion	317	1.54	0.89	1	5
	Experience of job discrimination based on religion	319	1.67	1.03	1	5
	Experience of some kind of discrimination but no complaint	316	1.88	1.17	1	5
Hate Ideology	Your religious beliefs being challenged by your work colleagues/school/college peers	326	2.36	1.15	1	5
	Witnessing or hearing Islamophobia	330	2.98	1.12	1	5
	Hearing Islamophobic comments made in particular by politicians or high ranking officials	329	3.78	1.12	1	5
	Witnessing politicians philosophize that Islam and Muslims are innately problematic	328	3.93	1.06	1	5
	Seeing negative or insulting stereotypes of Muslim people in the media (news, TV, etc.)	328	4.03	1.05	1	5
Hate practice	Experiences of physical assault	319	1.18	0.5	1	5
	Experiences of verbal abuse	317	1.84	0.95	1	5
	Being overlooked, ignored or denied service in a public office/ places	320	1.86	0.93	1	5
	Being treated with suspicion	318	2.03	1.04	1	5
	Being treated in an superficial manner	314	2.13	1.1	1	5
	Being talked down to	316	2.16	1.15	1	5
	Hearing an offensive joke or comment concerning Muslim people or about Islam	317	2.54	1.11	1	5
	Being stared at by strangers	318	2.55	1.27	1	5

Descriptive statistics of the different types of hate crime in the US (Ameli et al., 2013), the UK (Ameli et al., 2011; Ameli and Merali, 2015), Canada (Ameli and Merali, 2014), and France (Ameli, Merali and Shahghasemi, 2012) reflecting the correlations between the types of hate crime

Comparing the results of the experience of all types of hate crimes at a glance shows the relative severity of each experience compared to the others. It also highlights the extent to which Muslim citizens' views on each hate experience concur or differ. It is clear that the participants most agree with the statement 'those who discriminate against Muslims are highly targeted by the media content' (M = 4.28). This is an important point that shows Muslims perceive negative experience of hate crimes as a result of misrepresentation or negative representation by the mass media.

In contrast, as expected, the lowest intensity of hateful experience was related to 'experiences of physical assault' (M = 1.18). At the same time, it is important to keep in mind that this experience, despite its low severity, is more damaging in its short-term and long-term psychological, mental, and physical impact on victims.

In addition, all types of hate crimes are not homogeneous experiences, and therefore victims' experiences of each crime are not similar. Participants disagreed significantly (SD = 1.38) with each other about the statement 'those who discriminate against Muslims have an authentic picture of their religion'. In addition, their experience of being 'stared at by strangers' has a relatively higher prevalence (SD = 1.27) than other hate experiences. In contrast, their experience of 'physical assaults' was less dispersed than other experiences (SD = 0.5). The Muslim citizens' response to the statement 'experience of some kind of discrimination but afraid to complain' also has more convergence and less dispersion (SD = 0.82) than other cases.

Hate practices

In the hate practice category, there are eight statements including 'being overlooked, ignored or denied in a public office/places,' 'treated with suspicion,' 'being talked down to,' 'being treated in a superficial manner,' 'hearing an offensive joke or comment on Muslim people or about Islam,' 'being stared at by strangers,' 'experiences of verbal abuse,' and 'experiences of physical assault,' representing a wide range of hate practices from symbolic (being overlooked, ignored or denied) to physical violence (physical assault).

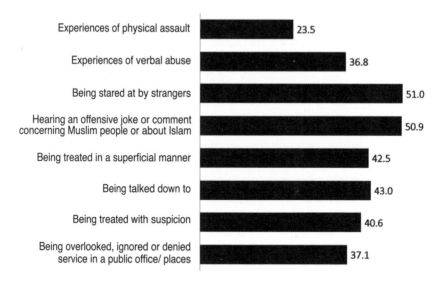

Experiences of physical assault	23.5
Experiences of verbal abuse	36.8
Being stared at by strangers	51.0
Hearing an offensive joke or comment concerning Muslim people or about Islam	50.9
Being treated in a superficial manner	42.5
Being talked down to	43.0
Being treated with suspicion	40.6
Being overlooked, ignored or denied service in a public office/ places	37.1

The intensity of hate crimes experienced in everyday life

As can be seen, the highest rate of hate crimes is related to 'being stared at by strangers' with 51 percent and then hearing offensive jokes (50.9 percent). At the same time, it should be noted that these different kinds of hate crimes are not the same in terms of significance, and therefore there is little difficulty in comparing them. For example, we know that 'physical assault' is more damaging than 'being overlooked.' Therefore, while the intensity of physical assaults is 23.5 percent, it represents a higher level of violence based on hate crimes.

Hate ideology

Under the hate ideology group, five variables have been evaluated, including 'witnessing or hearing about Islamophobia,' 'your religious beliefs being challenged by your work colleagues/school/college peers,' 'hearing Islamophobic comments made in particular by politicians or high ranking officials,' 'seeing negative or insulting stereotypes of Muslim people in the media (news, TV, etc.),' and 'witnessing politicians philosophize that Islam and Muslims are innately problematic.'

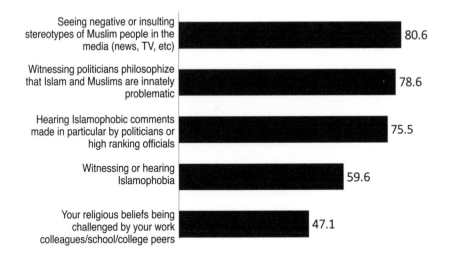

The intensity of hate crimes in the hate ideology group

'Seeing negative or insulting stereotypes of Muslim people in the media' (80.6 percent) has the highest frequency of hate crimes. After that, 'witnessing politicians are philosophizing that Islam and Muslims are innately problematic' with 78.6 percent, which is again one of the most extreme cases in this hate crimes set. The lowest level of hate crimes in this group relates to 'your religious beliefs being challenged by your work colleagues/school/college peers'with 47.1 percent.

Hate as discrimination

In this group, two statements of 'experience of job discrimination based on religion' and 'experience of educational discrimination based on religion' examine the hate experience in the work and educational environments respectively. Two other propositions, 'experience of some kind of discrimination but afraid to complain' and 'experience of some kind of discrimination but no complaint,' measure the degree of discrimination in terms of fear of judicial follow-up or unwillingness to pursue it.

The intensity of hate crimes in the group of hate as discrimination

In general, a comparative study shows that this group of hate crimes is not as strong in these results. However, discrimination in the work environment and discrimination in the educational environment are 33.3 percent and 30.7 percent respectively, which is statistically significant.

Hate representation

The group of questions about hate representation, consist of three statements, 'those who discriminate against Muslims have an authentic picture about them and their religion,' 'those who discriminate against Muslims are highly driven by media content' and 'if people know more about Muslims, they would act much better than the way they do now,' which measures the views of the participants on the reasons for the hate representation.

The intensity of hate crimes in the group of hate representation

In the group of hate representation, the highest score relates to the two statements: 'they would act much better than the way they do now,' and 'those who discriminate against Muslims are highly driven by media content,' which are 85.5 percent and 83.9 percent respectively. Therefore, in Muslims' view, these two issues have a tremendous significance in the development of hate crimes.

Hate policy

Finally, in the hate policy group, the four statements explicitly assess the attitudes of participants on the effect of hateful policies against Muslims, including 'discriminatory acts against Muslims are condoned by politicians,' 'politicians do not care about Muslims,' 'seeing policies or practices at work or school negatively affect Muslim people' and 'seeing political policies (local or national) that negatively affected Muslim people.'

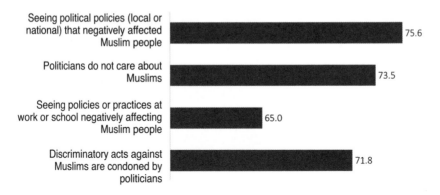

The intensity of hate crimes in the group of hate policy

In this group, in all cases, participants reported high levels of hate crimes. In other words, Muslim minorities largely understand hate crimes considered in hate politics.

From the viewpoint of the effect of demographic variables on the attitude variables, there are some cases of significant correlation. As shown in the table below, the gender and geographical position (in terms of the Muslim population's share in the neighborhood) affects hate practice. Males more than females (with a strong correlation of 0.263) and Muslims living in areas with a minority Muslim population are less likely to face this form of hate crime than people living in majority Muslim population areas.

In addition, the four demographic variables of age, gender, marital status, and work status have proven to have an impact on the hate ideology. Young people understand hate ideology more than older people (correlation intensity is 0.195). In addition, males are more likely to perceive this type of hate crime than females (correlation intensity of 0.208) and single adults more than married (correlation intensity of 0.182). In addition, the effect of work status shows that unemployed and retired people more than employed people understand hate ideology.

Another basic assumption is that victims of hate crimes do not have the same experience of tolerating hate crimes, depending on their individual characteristics such as gender, age, Islamic appearance etc. Analytically, it is expected that sociodemographic variables will influence the severity of these crimes. To test this hypothesis, we first need to take a look at the correlations between the sociodemographic variables and the different types of hate crimes.

	Hate practice		Hate ideology		Hate as discrimination		Hate representation		Hate policy	
	β	P	β	P	β	P	β	P	β	P
Age	-0.11	0.07	-0.2	0	0.06	0.34	0.07	0.23	-0.04	0.47
Gender	0.26	0	0.21	0	0	0.96	0.01	0.85	0.14	0.02
Marital status	-0.11	0.05	-0.18	0	0.02	0.79	0.03	0.59	-0.03	0.61
Proportion of Muslims in neighborhood	-0.09	0.14	-0.1	0.09	-0.06	0.33	-0.13	0.03	-0.07	0.22
Income group	-0.1	0.1	0.08	0.18	-0.18	0	-0.07	0.21	-0.03	0.59
Education	-0.05	0.38	-0.02	0.75	-0.01	0.94	-0.03	0.68	0.05	0.44
Work status	0.09	0.13	0.12	0.03	-0.02	0.75	-0.08	0.15	0.04	0.48
Being visibly Muslim	0.17	0	0.05	0.38	0.09	0.15	0.05	0.37	0.01	0.86
Religiosity	-0.06	0.33	-0.02	0.76	-0.01	0.91	0.07	0.27	0.07	0.24

Note: Regression coefficients are standardized. Cell entries are final-entry ordinary least squares (OLS) standardized coefficient.

Simple linear regression analysis of hate crime types

The regression analysis partially demonstrates the above assumption. Sociodemographic variables have the most impact on the experience of hate practice and hate ideology. Among sociodemographic variables, the effect of marital status on age is consistent. Thus, it can be understood that marital status does not affect the severity of the crime experience, but rather the observed correlation only happens due to the correlation between age and marital status. Overall, in examining the effect of sociodemographic variables on different types of hate crimes, there are some specific correlations that can support better understanding of the situation.

The two variables of economic situation and work sector affect hate as discrimination. Individuals in lower economic classes have experienced more discrimination based on their religion than those of the upper classes ($\beta=0.18$) and public sector employees more than private sector employees ($\beta=0.15$).

Hate representation and the hate policy are influenced by the place of living and gender, respectively. In the case of hate representation, it has been proven that people living in areas with less Muslim populations understand hate representation in the mass media more than those who living in higher-Muslim population areas ($\beta=0.12$). In addition, in the case of hate policy, males understand this particular type of hatred more than females ($\beta=0.14$).

The age variable affects all the propositions of hate ideology, and this relationship has always been indirect. In other words, young people more than adults understand the forms of hate ideology. The gender variable was affective in all of the variables in all five groups. In all cases, males more than females have perceived different forms of hate crimes.

In contrast with the other hate crime studies, education level has not had a significant impact on the experience of hate crimes. In other words, everyone, regardless of his or her educational level, understands hate crimes similarly. This situation, unexpectedly, also occurred for two other demographic variables, 'the extension of being visibly Muslim' and 'religiosity.' While studies mainly show the broad effect of these two variables on the hate crimes experiences, in the present study, these two variables have limited effects. The only visible effect of the extension of being visibly Muslim has been 'being stared at by strangers' ($\beta=0.31$), which indicates that having the appearance of a Muslim has increased the likelihood of encountering this special kind of hate crime. This variable has been ineffective in other cases.

In addition, religiosity has an effect on two variables: 'Hearing an offensive joke or comment on Muslim people or about Islam' ($\beta=0.18$) and 'if people know more about Muslims, they would act much better than the way they do now' ($\beta=0.18$). In the first case, this is indirect, which shows that the more religious one is, the lower the exposure to this auditory experience. In the second case, the relation is direct and shows that by increasing the religiosity level, the likelihood of his consent to the second proposition will be greater.

Previous studies of hate crimes against Muslims in other countries[2] show that there is a strong correlation between the types of experienced hate crimes. These correlations have also been addressed through broad theoretical approaches, including structuralist as well as action-oriented approaches to social and cultural issues. Are the assumed correlations between the different types of hate crimes also true in this data?

	Hate practice	Hate ideology	Hate as discrimination	Hate representation
Hate ideology	0.44**			
Hate as discrimination	0.58**	0.28*		
Hate representation	0.04	0.08	0.07	
Hate policy	0.38**	0.45**	0.36**	0.14*

Intensity of correlation between different types of hate crimes

Except hate representation, other types of hate crimes are strongly correlated with each other. At the same time, hate representation is only marginally related to hate policy (the intensity of correlation = 0.14). It is therefore clear that the experience of all types of hate crimes coincides. If so, the next question is how the variables within each of the hate crime types are related. In addition, what does this kind of probabilistic relationship have to do with sociodemographic variables? To answer these questions, extensive tests were performed using hierarchical regression analysis. The following set of cases that predict the existence of correlation is used in this analysis.

---

[2] The extensive evidence of hate crime studies in the USA (Ameli et al., 2013), the UK (Ameli et al., 2011; Ameli and Merali, 2015), Canada (Ameli and Merali, 2014), and France (Ameli et al., 2012) reflect the correlations between the types of hate crime.

	Hate practice	
	β	P
Sociodemographic characteristics		
Gender	0.19	0.00
The extension of being visibly Muslim	0.17	0.00
Affective hate experiences		
Your beliefs being challenged by your work colleagues/school/college peers	0.12	0.08
Experience of job discrimination based on religion	0.11	0.16
Experience of some kind of discrimination but afraid to complain	0.16	0.02
Experience of some kind of discrimination but no complaint	0.21	0.00

Note: Regression coefficients are standardized. Cell entries are final-entry ordinary least squares (OLS) standardized coefficients. Multi-collinearity was checked.

Hierarchical regression analysis of hate practice

It is clear that the experience of hate practice is most likely to occur for people who did not complain ($\beta = 0.21$) or fear judicial prosecution if they experienced some form of religious discrimination ($\beta = 0.16$). There are those who experience greater discrimination at work ($\beta = 0.11$) and are also more sensitive to identifying belief challenges in the workplace or school ($\beta = 0.12$). It is observed that males have more experience of hate practice than females ($\beta = 0.19$) and also those who are visibly Muslim more than the others ($\beta = 0.17$).

	Hate practice	
	β	P
Sociodemographic characteristics		
The proportion of Muslims in the neighborhood	-0.13	0.07
Income	-0.14	0.05
Affective hate experiences		
Being overlooked, ignored or denied service in a public office/ places	0.11	0.28
Being talked down to	-0.11	0.39
Hearing an offensive joke or comment concerning Muslim people or about Islam	0.18	0.06
Your religious beliefs being challenged by your work colleagues/school/college peers	-0.15	0.12
Seeing negative or insulting stereotypes of Muslim people in the media (news, TV, etc.)	0.13	0.33
Experience of educational discrimination based on religion	-0.15	0.12
Experience of some kind of discrimination but afraid to complain	0.16	0.11
Discriminatory acts against Muslims are condoned by politicians	0.21	0.01
Seeing policies or practices at work or school negatively affect Muslim people	-0.11	0.20

Note: Regression coefficients are standardized. Cell entries are final-entry ordinary least squares (OLS) standardized coefficients. Multi-collinearity was checked.

Hierarchical regression analysis of hate representation

In analyzing the variables affecting the hate representation experience, it is important to pay attention to the negative correlations. In other words, it is clear that increasing specific hate experiences will lead to a decrease in the perception of negative media representation of Muslims. Among these experiences, the experience of challenging religious beliefs by colleagues or others at school and the experience of religious-based academic discrimination are those that have the most negative impact (β=-0.15) on hate representation experience. Conversely, the belief that 'discriminatory acts against Muslims are condoned by politicians' has a positive effect (β=0.21) on the experience of hate representation. It is also clear that the percentage of Muslim neighbors and the amount of income a person has had a negative impact on his or her hate representation experience. In other words, people living in neighborhoods with smaller Muslim populations (β=-0.13) and those with lower income levels (β=-0.14) experience greater levels of hate representation. Extensive experiences of other types of hate crimes have a growing influence on the hate experience, most notably the beliefs of 'discriminatory acts against Muslims being condoned by politicians' (β=0.21) and 'hearing an offensive joke or comment concerning Muslim people or about Islam' (β=0.18).

	Hate practice	
	β	P
Sociodemographic characteristics		
Age	-0.09	0.15
Income	0.06	0.29
Affective hate experiences		
Being overlooked, ignored or denied service in a public office/ places	-0.11	0.16
Being treated with suspicion	0.10	0.22
Being talked down to	0.19	0.06
Hearing an offensive joke or comment concerning Muslim people or about Islam	0.31	0.00
Being stared at by strangers	0.19	0.02
Experiences of verbal abuse	-0.28	0.00
Experience of job discrimination based on religion	0.12	0.16
Those who discriminate against Muslims are highly driven by the media content	0.11	0.08
Discriminatory acts against Muslims are condoned by politicians	0.11	0.07
Politicians do not care about Muslims	0.10	0.13
Seeing political policies (local or national) that negatively affect Muslim people	0.18	0.01

Note: Regression coefficients are standardized. Cell entries are final-entry ordinary least squares (OLS) standardized coefficients. Multi-collinearity was checked.

Hierarchical regression analysis of hate ideology

Experiences that influence the intensity of hate ideology are very broad, encompassing both a negative and a positive impact. Among the experiences that have an increasing impact on the experience of hate ideology, 'hearing an offensive joke or comment on Muslim people' (β=0.31), 'being talked down to' (β=0.19), 'being stared at by strangers. (β=0.19) and 'seeing political policies that negatively affected Muslim people' (β = 0.18) were more effective. In contrast, 'experiences of verbal abuse' (β=-0.28) is an experience that has the greatest deterrent effect on hate ideology. In addition, hate ideology experiences are slightly higher among young people than in older people (β=-0.09) and slightly more among upper-class individuals (β=0.06).

	Hate practice	
	β	P
Sociodemographic characteristics		
Gender	0.08	0.17
Being visibly Muslim	0.13	0.02
Income	-0.08	0.14
Affective hate experiences		
Being overlooked, ignored or denied service in a public office/ places	0.12	0.07
Being stared at by strangers	-0.15	0.05
Experiences of verbal abuse	0.21	0.01
Experiences of physical assault	0.11	0.05
Your religious beliefs being challenged by your work colleagues/school/college peers	0.15	0.02
Seeing negative or insulting stereotypes of Muslim people in the media (news, TV, etc)	-0.13	0.15
Those who discriminate against Muslims have an authentic picture about them and their religion	0.18	0.00
Politicians do not care about Muslims	0.13	0.02
Seeing policies or practices at work or school negatively affect Muslim people	0.18	0.00

Note: Regression coefficients are standardized. Cell entries are final-entry ordinary least squares (OLS) standardized coefficients. Multi-collinearity was checked.

Hierarchical regression analysis of hate as discrimination

Hate as discrimination, like hate ideology, is influenced by different types of hate experiences. However, the severity of the impact of these experiences on hate as discrimination experience is not strong. Among the positive affective experiences, 'experiences of verbal abuse' (β=0.21) had the greatest effect on enhancing the experience of discrimination. In addition, among the experiences that have a deterrent effect on hate as discrimination experience, 'being stared at by strangers' has the highest inhibitory effect (β=-0.15). Being visibly Muslim (β=0.13) also had a more pronounced effect on hate as discrimination among sociodemographic variables.

	Hate practice	
	β	P
Sociodemographic characteristics		
Gender	0.08	0.27
Religiosity	0.07	0.26
Affective hate experiences		
Being treated with suspicion	0.12	0.19
Witnessing politicians philosophize that Islam and Muslims are innately problematic	0.16	0.15
Experience of educational discrimination based on religion	0.12	0.13
Experience of some kind of discrimination but no complaint	0.26	0.00
Those who discriminate against Muslims have an authentic picture about them and their religion	-0.12	0.06
Those who discriminate against Muslims are highly driven by the media content	0.11	0.11
If people know more about Muslims, they would act much better than the way they do now	0.14	0.04

Note: Regression coefficients are standardized. Cell entries are final-entry ordinary least squares (OLS) standardized coefficients. Multi-collinearity was checked.

Hierarchical regression analysis of hate policy

Among the different types of hate crimes, there is a difference between the type of hate policy experience and the extent to which Muslims understand it, compared to other types of hate crimes. Hate policy is mainly covered in more hidden but more effective formats (in terms of scope and duration of impact). Hate policy against Islam, in particular, may not be recognizable by citizens as hate crime because of the specific support it receives from political ideologies in western societies.

However, the results of this study indicate a high sensitivity of Muslim citizens to this particular type of hate crime. The relatively high level of hate policy experience announced by survey participants is a strong reason to show Muslims are sensitive to this type of hatred. On the other hand, the intensity of the hate policy experience is influenced by the experience of some types of hate crimes. This type of hatred experience is profoundly influenced by 'experience of some kind of discrimination but no complaint' ($\beta=0.26$). Other types of experiences have similarly more limited effects on hate policy. Among the experiences affecting the hate policy experience, the belief that 'those who discriminate against Muslims have an authentic picture about their religion' has a decreasing effect (β=-0.12) on the intensity of the hate policy experience.

Each type of hate crime has distinct differences with the other types. However, there is a strong correlation between these different types of crimes, and as a result, the exposure of Muslim citizens to each type of hate crime correlates with increased experience of other types of hate. At the same time, the results of this study show that US Muslim citizens are more likely to experience hate speech as represented in the mass media than to experience it as a practice. This situation may be related to the powerful effect of mass media across this country. However, such a claim needs more extensive study and research.

Chapter 6

Policy
Recommendations

Muslim Americans recognize the pervasive and threatening nature of Islamophobia in the United States. They are right, and within their rights, to seek recourse from the US government to ameliorate the situation and the dangers their community faces on a daily basis. Yet, the American government has a troubled history with accepting both responsibility and recommendations to rectify social distress. In the midst of the 1967 Detroit disturbances, brought on by the frustrations of decades-long policies of systematic and institutional racism, President Lyndon Johnson convened the Kerner Commission to investigate and recommend critical policy changes to correct causal factors, both in the city as well as in other parts of the United States, to prevent a recurrence. The Commission proffered a series of cogent recommendations after identifying the root cause of the discord, i.e. barriers to socio-economic well-being as a result of rampant structural racism in education, service sectors and housing. The 462-page report became a national best seller, and recommended wide sweeping changes to existing government policy in these areas that, if implemented, could significantly improve the conditions for African Americans. (United States, 1980) Unfortunately, President Johnson rejected the findings and recommendations as being a personal attack on his administration and a rebuke of his efforts to make progress under his hallmark Civil Rights Act of 1964 and Voting Rights Act of 1965. (United States, 1969) As a result, the racial divide in the country greatly expanded, as did the further entrenchment of structural racism.

Muslim Americans have to contend with the realization that Islamophobia is a manifestation of the entrenched structural racism in the United States. While it is critical for them to delineate and highlight the need for significant policy changes to curb the toxicity of anti-Muslim bigotry, Muslims must be mindful that the government may be uncooperative to implement such changes, especially when they are responsible for creating, perpetuating and profiting from the conditions for that bigotry. Nonetheless, the following are a series of sectors where the community ought to focus its attention for the deployment of Islamophobia as well as strategies to combat its threatening effects.

Judicial Challenges
Constitutionality

One of the most effective ways of combating anti-Muslim hatred is to avail oneself of the judicial system. An increasingly common strategy in the courts is to challenge the constitutionality of various anti-mosque and anti-sharia legislation. For example, zoning laws and ordinances have been liberally applied as ways to prevent Muslim American communities from establishing and/or expanding their respective Islamic institutions, including mosques, schools and even Muslim cemeteries. The ploy of arguing that Muslim facilities are violating public use parameters represents a cynical effort to reduce the Muslim presence within the broader public sphere of the communities in which they reside. Often times, such attacks on Muslim communities reek of hypocrisy given that other religious communities are not placed or subjected to similar scrutiny. A frequent complaint levelled against Muslim communities is the traffic congestion that accompanies Muslim services, especially Friday prayer. Of course, no such nuisance is alleged during church services on Sundays. It is true that Muslim communities in America are still relatively young compared to those of other religious faiths, consequently, they are still in the process of establishing the institutions necessary to meet community demand. Churches, synagogues and parochial schools may have maintained a presence for centuries while mosques and other Muslim facilities are, in most cases, barely decades old. As Muslim Americans further integrate into broader society, they are merely following a trajectory that every other religion has done in the country. It is true that in America's recent past, other faiths have endured discrimination and similar obstacles to their development of necessary institutions, a case in point being the Catholic community in the early 20th century. Similarly, many of the challenges to Muslim American facility establishment, while cloaked in legal arguments, expose naked xenophobia and bigotry.

In 2018, a Syrian American Muslim group purchased some land in the Detroit suburb of Sterling Heights, Michigan, with the intention of constructing a new mosque on the site. The effort was met with considerable opposition from the city's immigrant Iraqi Christian (Chaldean) community, which argued that the new facility would greatly increase traffic and congestion along the adjacent roads. Despite evidence presented by the mosque officials showing limited increase in traffic, the city council rejected the Muslims' application. The mosque officials elected to avail themselves of the courts, bringing a lawsuit against the City of Sterling Heights in the Federal Court, under the Religious Land Use and Institutionalized Persons Act (RUILPA), a federal law that seeks to protect religious communities and institutions from excessive overreach and/or discrimination efforts by government entities. (United States, 2000) The courts ruled in favor of the Syrian American Muslim plaintiffs, on the grounds that the city had in fact violated their civil rights under RUILPA.

Similar efforts to prevent the establishment of Muslim American institutions occurred in Murfreesboro, Tennessee, a city close to the state capital, Nashville. Home to Middle Tennessee State University and no stranger to international students and faculty of Muslim heritage, Murfreesboro had a small permanent Muslim community, much of it tied in some way to the university. As the community sought to build a mosque and a Muslim cemetery, it was confronted by blistering opposition from not only many townspeople, but also a concerted, coordinated network of special interest groups from across the country that considered Murfreesboro a line in the sand to repel perceived Muslim encroachment.

The campaign to block mosque construction became very contentious, polarizing Murfreesboro between those who supported the Muslim effort and those who were virulently against any foothold being established by Muslim Americans in this Bible Belt town. The mosque site was subject to arson, and community members faced a variety of threats, ranging from the relatively mild to life-threatening. But the public acrimony was matched by the sparks in the courtroom. A lawyer representing the mosque's opponents even made the audacious argument that Islam was not a legitimate religion and thus ineligible to receive constitutional protection. The Attorney General of the United States, Eric Holder, intervened in the case when it issued a statement on behalf of the Obama administration giving judicial notice that Islam was indeed a recognized religion. That the US government had to proffer a statement of determination for a 14-centuries-old faith, with a population of 1.8 billion worldwide and 3.5 million domestically, stretched the limits of absurdity. Nonetheless, the President and his agencies felt the imperative to act accordingly. Ultimately, the Muslims of Murfreesboro prevailed by invoking RUIPLA.

In the past two decades, over 35 states across the United States have attempted to pass legislation that bans consideration or application of sharia law in judicial proceedings or affords it public recognition. The first such case occurred in 2010 in the state of Oklahoma. The challenge to the enacted law was based on a First Amendment argument that the legislation, as written, was vague and overbroad, and unduly restrictive of the free exercise of religion. In addition, such laws were utterly unnecessary and prophylactic as there was no threat of any effort to have sharia law being codified within the purview of American jurisprudence. Similar challenges in other states all yielded victories for the Muslim community, as court after court struck down these laws as unconstitutional.

Early defeats for the anti-sharia warriors were hardly a deterrent to subsequent legislative efforts to ban sharia with all bills following a single template that had initially been drafted by an Islamophobe. The political exploitation of the general public by creating a false hysteria of a phantom menace – sharia - was effective in allowing bigoted politicians to raise campaign funds and potential re-election on an Islamophobic platform. In addition, these frivolous legislative efforts were particularly enervating to Muslim communities across the country that had to expend precious and limited resources to challenge them in the courts. They diverted Muslim communities' resources away from internal investment.

Non-Religious Related Legal Issues as Actionable Legal Strategies

In the current socio-political climate in the United States, the Muslim-American community is not alone in being the target of bigotry. Hatred is an intersectional phenomenon. The attacks against Muslims are often not solely an issue of religious freedom; they also relate to a host of legal matters, including gender, civil rights, economic harm and defamation/slander. They also affect other constitutional issues such as equal protection, due process and fundamental rights. Lastly, civil rights issues, such as those covered by the American Civil Liberties Union (ACLU), including employment discrimination, immigration, social media monitoring, CVE and watchlists all warrant developing multi-faceted legal strategies. Such an approach has the impact of raising awareness and contextuality to allow broader society to relate to the challenges facing Muslim Americans because many of those areas of violation could affect them as well. It is also a potential gateway to coalition building with other suspect groups that have to confront various forms of hatred and discrimination.

Challenging Executive Orders

Legislative action, whether at the local, state or federal level, is not the only form of governmental attack on Muslim Americans. There has been a disturbing increase in the power of the executive branch, and especially the presidential use of the executive order. Generally, the White House will avail itself of the executive order as a means of circumventing the normal channels of the legislative process because it might be too time consuming or yield an outcome that is antithetical to the President's policy objectives on a particular issue. A legislative bill could be defeated by a veto, but Congress can still override the presidential veto and enact the bill into law. An executive order that may be declared could be declared unconstitutional by the courts, just like a law, and can also be nullified by a subsequent president or a legislative act, making for an easier process of nullification. Nonetheless, the executive order can wield a tremendous level of power and authority during its period of enforcement. Perhaps the strongest illustration of this reality is the 2017 executive order signed by President Donald Trump that restricts entry to the United States from a series of countries, most of which are Muslim majority nations, i.e. the so-called travel ban or Muslim ban. The first executive order on the matter occurred exactly one week to the day Trump took the oath of office, fulfilling a campaign promise he made as one that he would ban Muslims from entering the United States. Anticipating the release of the much-publicized action, Muslim Americans mobilized with a wide array of allies and opponents to perceived presidential overreach by organizing mass protests and demonstrations at airports and other public spaces. The coalition that came together included people and organizations representing every segment of American society ethnically, religiously and even ideologically. Some conservatives in fact voiced their opposition to the ban as being patently un-American and an egregious abuse of presidential power.

The Trump travel ban was also immediately challenged in the federal courts, where opponents received an injunction that temporarily prevented the ban from going into implementation, pending the White House's appeals process. The judicial maneuvers forced the White House to modify the ban on at least two additional occasions, anticipating that modifications would pass legal scrutiny; they did not, and consequently, the issue was decided by the United States Supreme Court in *Trump v Hawai'i* (2018). Despite Trump's numerous proclamations that he was in fact seeking to target Muslims (notwithstanding his amateurish efforts to demonstrate that the ban was broader by including countries like North Korea and Venezuela), the United States Supreme Court gave tremendous deference to the Executive Branch and held that the President's actions were constitutional. The Court reasoned that the constitutional principle of the separation of powers allowed the President to make decisions regarding immigration, especially if they pertained to national security. Such an authority, although presumptively granted to a President who would exercise such powers in good faith and without discriminating against a specific group, does not have any constitutional provisos to that effect, and the Supreme Court was reluctant to place such a requirement upon another, co-equal branch of the government.

Although not ultimately successful in blocking President Trump's exploitation of executive power, Muslim Americans could seek some solace in recognizing that opposition to a government action targeting them was championed by a strong, vocal and mobilized coalition of Americans who recognized the corrosive effect such abuse of presidential authority would have on the country and on the public's perception of its government and rule of law. While the Supreme Court's decision was entirely predictable, even dreaded by scholars and observers of American constitutional law, the large and vociferous public opposition to the travel ban caused the Trump administration to reconsider the wording and scope of the original executive order on at least two additional occasions, suggesting their own diffidence in the merits and viability of their action. While successful judicially, the court of public opinion certainly pronounced a different verdict. That Americans representing a broad spectrum of the body politic took on the Muslim plight as their own cause célèbre was a case study in the potential and power of civic engagement through coalition building, whether formally or as a matter of circumstance. Given the obsessive nature of politicians to voter polls, presidents do pay attention to issues and actions that defy and deviate strongly from what the public may be willing to accept during a future election cycle. The announcement by the White House of the expansion of the travel ban to include more countries in early 2020 shows the cynical exploitation of xenophobia that the President hopes to leverage among his voter base ahead of his bid for re-election. Given the absence of judicial support the election also allows for yet another opportunity for the Muslim American community and the coalition of ban opponents to remobilize to reverse an executive order using the ballot box.

Legislative Action
Blocking Negative Bills and Laws

Anti-sharia legislation of some kind has been sponsored in 43 out of the 50 states within the past 10 years alone, according to the Southern Poverty Law Center. (Southern Poverty Law Center, 2020) Fortunately, none of these bills has survived constitutional challenge in the courts. At the same time, it is important to remember that Texas and Arkansas were successful in enacting the bills into law, before facing a judicial battle to nullify them. Courts thus far have proved reliable in overturning noxious legislation that clearly is discriminatory and in violation of the US Constitution. But the court system has undergone a profound change in the past few years under the Trump Administration, with full complicity of an ambitious, Republican majority Senate, whereby conservative judges have been appointed to fill hundreds of vacancies at the district court and appellate court levels. Moreover, the Supreme Court enjoys a conservative majority, thanks to severe manipulation of the political process by Senate Majority Leader Mitch McConnell. These judges and justices have lifetime appointments and could just as easily overturn past precedent and interpretations of the Constitution to consider anti-sharia laws as perfectly acceptable within the American legal canon. As such, efforts must be made to prevent such legislation from even receiving a vote in the various state legislatures.

Generally, anti-sharia and other anti-Muslim legislation is financed and supported by a small, but powerful minority that seeks to enflame and exploit people's fears and bigotry, something that willing politicians manipulate for votes and campaign contributions. There is an inverse relationship between the efforts to pass anti-sharia/anti-Muslim legislation in a particular state and the number of Muslims residing there. It suggests that there is a political calculation being made that Muslim Americans lack the social and political capital to launch a successful counter campaign to the legislative efforts given the size of their community. Similarly, efforts by Muslim Americans to promote legislation that protects them, their communities and their civil liberties are often rebuffed as unnecessary or even potentially toxic by politicians who would prefer to shun Muslims lest they be seen as sympathetic and interested in protecting their civil rights. Whether seeking to block negative legislation or promote positive laws, Muslim Americans recognize that at approximately 1% of the total US population, their political footprint can only be enhanced through coalition building with other empathetic and potentially affected groups, many of whom have considerable experience and resources already deployed within this political and legislative space.

Combatting Toxic Rhetoric and Discrimination
Political Speech

Anti-Muslim speech has now been weaponized by politicians, both at the national and local levels, as a means of appealing to nativistic, xenophobic and bigoted sentiments and impulses. President Trump has stated that, "Islam hates us" and has demonstrated his xenophobia through the various incarnations of his so-called travel bans, with the vast majority of the countries targeted being Muslim majority nations. Similarly, politicians in the state legislature and even local officials have impugned Muslims as a collective, branding them as terrorists or potential terrorists, and even questioned whether their values are compatible with American society. According to the Survey of Muslim Experiences of Hatred, Hostility and Discrimination , 78.6% of Muslims stated that they had witnessed politicians philosophize that Islam and Muslims are inherently problematic, and 75.5% had heard Islamophobic comments being made in particular by politicians or high-ranking officials.

Due to the constitutional protections of free speech, particularly political speech, politicians speaking in their official capacity effectively enjoy an absolute immunity from prosecution or accountability for what they say, irrespective of tone and toxicity. Absent speech that could be deemed defamatory, politicians can speak with impunity, regardless of the consequences, such as inflaming people's hatred even to the point of acting against suspect communities. Politicians are adept enough to avoid directly slanderous speech as it involves falsity about a specific individual. However, group disparagement, even if mendacious, is not legally actionable. Politicians are also careful to avoid rhetoric which could be seen as a direct incitement to violence.

Words translate into policy, and many Muslim Americans perceive a correlation between politicians' toxic rhetoric against their community and policies which target them. 75.6% of Muslim Americans surveyed see political policies, either at the local or national level, that negatively affect Muslim people. In similar numbers (73.5%), Muslim Americans believe that politicians simply do not care about Muslims. Again, this suggests the recognition that Muslims lack the social and political capital to be considered a viable and important constituency in the United States. Perhaps worse, 71.8% of Muslim Americans believe that discriminatory acts against Muslims that are committed by members of the public or government officials are condoned by these politicians, creating a sense of despair that their elected representatives do not have their best interests, welfare and protection in mind.

The optimal way to countermand toxic speech from politicians is mass, grassroots mobilization, involving not only Muslim Americans but also other advocacy groups. In the current political and cultural landscape, Muslim Americans are not the only group to be targeted by bigoted politicians. It is critical to marshal support and voice from a large coalition of supporters who can condemn such hate-filled rhetoric and make politicians reconsider and/or retract their statements. As politicians only understand money and votes, they need to be appraised of the fact that their speech can cost them more of both than they stand to gain.

In the United States, there is perhaps no stronger message to send a politician in registering one's discontent and disapproval of their rhetoric than to prevent his/her election or re-election. While special interest groups, including Islamophobic entities, wield tremendous influence on electoral campaigns by contributing millions of dollars to politicians' candidacies, the United States is still a one person, one vote system. Voting against a particular politician is certainly effective, as is support of his/her opponent, either at the primary level or during the general election. This strategy to remove a noxious politician can be facilitated by coalition building to assert the consequences of bigoted speech and policies.

In addition to efforts to reduce the number of bigoted politicians in public office, the dual track strategy of coalition building to oppose noxious policy is a critical complement. There are growing examples across the United States where such coalition building has affected and even reversed noxious policies that target the Muslim American community. In New York City, Muslims in 2013 joined forces with over 60 organizations representing a broad spectrum of communities and activist causes to severely and successfully curtail the city's "Stop and Frisk" and Muslim surveillance programs, which disproportionately targeted and impacted Muslims and people of color. The coalition was able to persuade city council members to pass legislation that countermanded both programs, fortifying the vote to withstand even a mayoral veto. (Beutel and Jankovic, 2015)

In another example of effective coalition building, the Muslim community of Murfreesboro, Tennessee formed several civic organizations as well as a coalition with allies from other communities to oppose campaigns directed at anti-sharia and anti-mosque legislation. (Beutel and Jankovic, 2015) The united presence of such a coalition demonstrated to legislators that the opposition to such laws did not just reside within the relatively small Muslim community. That others empathized and showed solidarity with a beleaguered community sent a powerful message that politicians and bigots would be held accountable for their trafficking of suppressive policies. This deterrent effect is perhaps best illustrated during the reaction to the 2017 travel ban in which thousands of Americans of all backgrounds protested at several airports across the country. The potential of a policy that primarily targeted Muslims to mobilize and organize people to civic action did not go unnoticed by politicians, especially those who closely aligned themselves to President Trump. During the 2018 midterm elections, few if any publicly expressed support for the travel bans in their campaigns for election or re-election.

Media

The media is far too vast and complex an entity to be able to cogently label as Islamophobic or not, per se. And yet, the sheer volume of anti-Muslim coverage is absorbed and internalized by Muslim-Americans. The Chicagoland SMEHHD survey shows that 80.6% of Muslims who were polled responded that they had seen negative or insulting stereotypes of Muslim people in the media.

There are certainly outlets that one can describe as fair and objectively their coverage of Muslim communities and issues. Yet, there are several that demonstrate a palpable hostility toward Muslim Americans, to the point of fabricating narratives and/or advancing known conspiracy theories designed to cast Muslims in a false and negative light. Right wing newspapers, cable television networks and talk radio have created a narrative that demonizes and dehumanizes Muslims and Islam. Their consumer base is quite large, tends to lean and vote on the conservative side of the spectrum and espouse the most virulent anti-Muslim hatred. Fox News, Tucker Carlson, Bill O'Reilly, Sean Hannity and Rush Limbaugh are a few of the most visible and consistent architects of the Islamophobia narrative within the media constellation.

But anti-Muslim narratives are not the exclusive domain of the American right-wing; Islamophobia is also deployed from the left, by so called "enlightened" liberals who see Islam and Muslims as culturally backward and through the lens of abject racism. Bill Maher, a comedian with his own panel show on cable television, frequently debases Islam and Muslims as being the worst example of people who subscribe to religion. A self-professed atheist, Maher only exhibits his contempt for faith and faith traditions by singling out Muslims and Islam, despite ample evidence of the dangerous diffusion and deep encroachment of Evangelical Christianity and its values into American civil and political life. He uses his talk show as a pulpit to disparage Muslims through mockery and/or trafficking the worst stereotypes about the community, its customs and Islam's teachings. If he does have Muslims as guests, they are either sycophantic informants (existing or ex-Muslims), who validate his assertions with their self-appointed Islamic imprimatur, or individuals specifically selected and invited because they trigger responses that play to his portrayal of Muslims as irrational and hypersensitive.

Even seemingly benign and respected media outlets perpetuate the dangerous stereotypes about Muslims and Islam. Mainstream news networks, in their zeal to fill 24-hour news cycles with "breaking news" exclusives, often presume that acts of violent extremism are committed by a Muslim actor and more so, that the motivation for such acts is religiously based. Islam seems to be the only religious tradition to which such an impetus is ascribed; no other suspect is identified by his/her religious affiliation, even when explicitly stated, as in the case of radical Christians, Hindus or even Buddhists of late. This is most evident in the use of the word, "terrorist," almost exclusively deployed when concerning a potential Muslim actor.

While recently, i.e. since the start of the Trump Administration, some media outlets have begun to "expand" the scope of the use of the word, "terrorist" to include white supremacists and white nationalists, whom law enforcement agencies now acknowledge a far bigger threat to American society than Muslim extremists, there is still the presumption that Muslims have to rebut that they are blameless for the act in question. This internalization of the Muslim as the "problem" and./or existential threat to American security is also felt by Muslim Americans, who shudder any time the media reports an act of extremism and mass killing. Muslims are left literally to pray that the suspect is not a Muslim, for fear of the inevitable backlash that will occur, via toxic rhetoric, government policy or vigilante acts of discrimination and retaliation.

The media's enormous and relatively unchecked power in shaping the narrative about Muslims is recognized fully by the Muslim American community. It explains why 85.5% in the SMEHHD reported that they believe those who discriminate against Muslims are highly driven by media content. The community is well aware of both the power and relative immunity the media enjoys in reporting content with editorial bias that casts Muslims as a convenient enemy, yet without any concern about the social implications of such "journalism." As the media is driven by two main motivations - profit margins and the "if it bleeds, it leads" axiom - accuracy and decency are easily compromised. These distortions correlate to action against the community; according to our survey, only 40.8% of Muslim Americans polled believe that those who discriminate against Muslims have an authentic picture about them and their religion, suggesting that having a genuine, truthful depiction of Muslims would reduce prejudice. It is worth reflecting upon the recommendations from the Kerner Report on the significant role the media plays in framing and even defining communities, especially involving people of colour. (United States, 1988) The report emphasized the need to have sufficient representation of suspect communities in all dimensions of media operations, including journalists and others who cover the news, especially of the community itself. In addition, the report suggests that there is a critical need for greater diversity and representation among editorial boards and media coverage, per se. Finally, there needs to be credible representation of Muslim Americans to have the opportunity to speak on all issues, rather than be passive tokens or props in coverage of their own community.

Although not an acknowledged media authority, internet opinion maker Alex Jones has admitted that he was responsible for disseminating several false anti-Muslim stories specifically to stoke hatred against Muslim Americans. He will face no significant retribution and certainly no criminal prosecution for his actions, even if some may have been inspired and motivated to commit hate crimes against Muslims.

As with the case of Alex Jones, the internet and social media are replete with some of the most toxic and virulent anti-Muslim rhetoric. One explanation for this is the stated reluctance for internet portals, e.g. Facebook, Twitter, Instagram, WhatsApp, to silence speech that might be hateful but not criminal. One of the main criticisms that has been levelled against these platforms is the alleged uneven policy implementation, where it appears as though hate speech directed at other groups is more readily and rapidly removed and/or blocked, while rhetoric targeting Muslims is allowed to fester, even thrive on these sites.

Combatting toxic media narratives about Muslim Americans requires a high level of vigilance and investigation of media outlets. Most importantly, it involves Muslims reclaiming the agency of their own narrative. Responses to negative coverage can be made on specific accounts through the comments section, although these are perilous spaces given the often virulent, unregulated remarks posted by individuals, whether real or generated, that sometimes have the unintended consequence of further inflaming the issue at hand. A better option is to insist from the media outlet in question space for advancing an alternative position. Usually, this can be achieved by writing an op-ed to be run on the outlet's editorial pages, whether in print or online. It is equally critical to cultivate relationships with journalists and editors of various outlets. It allows for greater visibility and for these individuals in the field to be aware of potential, viable and accurate sources for their journalism. Similarly, Muslim Americans should develop relationships with producers of news and other television shows where Muslims and Muslim issues are discussed in panel settings and insist on better representation of Muslims reflecting a boarder and more accurate segment of the community.

The development of such relationships with the media requires the Muslim American community to be mindful about the dynamics of the media as well as strategies to optimize the often limited opportunities for media engagement. The media in the aggregate might be considered a neutral entity but on the specific level, there is the reality of bias and slant. It is therefore essential to understand and devise methods to navigate a space that cannot be presumed to be "objective" or balanced. In addition, Muslim communities ought to devise a well-structured plan on whom to recommend to appear on the media, based upon their respective areas of expertise, eloquence and ability to manage sometimes hostile media outlets. It requires an acknowledgement, and humility, that community leaders may not be best equipped or suited to appear before the media.

Statistics matter. Muslim Americans should contribute to the public discourse, and the creation of their own narrative by proffering indisputable data about their community. There are now several organizations that provide solid statistical evidence, analysis and interpretation on a series of issues and perspectives regarding Muslim Americans. These can either be cited directly or recommended for others to consult on their own. ISPU, MPAC, Muslim Advocates and CAIR are just two of the organizations from within the Muslim American community that offer such valuable information, as do other organizations like the Pew Center and the Southern Poverty Law Center.

Another pernicious aspect of social media is the existence of bots, automated accounts that generate toxic content and direct it toward targeted audiences. Many of these bots spread misinformation regarding political issues but are also deployed to foment resentment and hatred of specific groups like Muslims. Again, despite efforts to demand action from social media platforms to monitor and remove such accounts, and notwithstanding pledges from such outlets to be vigilant, the widespread reach and adverse effect of bots remains. It is nonetheless imperative that the community insists that these platforms intensify their efforts to remove toxic bots and accounts from their platforms, especially as they violate their own stated policies.

Anti-Muslim hatred, whether promoted by politicians, shaped and amplified by the media or applied through government policies, has a corrosive impact on the Muslim American community. The hate experienced by them in everyday life varies in its intensity, is quite real and has devastating consequences in the amount of trauma it places upon not only the individual victim but also the whole community. Muslims find that they are subject to a litany of negative behaviors where the perceived cause is Islamophobia. In the Chicagoland survey, Muslims reported a wide variety of actions they consider directed against them because of their identity. 51% report being stared at by strangers, while nearly as many (50.9%) have heard an offensive comment concerning Muslims or Islam in their presence. 43% claim they have been on the receiving end of condescending conversation, while 42.5% say they have been treated in a superficial manner. 40.6% of Muslims have at some point been treated with suspicion, while 37.1% believe they have been overlooked, ignored or denied service in public settings due to their Muslim identity. On the more dangerous side of experiences, 36.8% report being subjected to verbal abuse, while 23.5% have encountered actual physical abuse for being Muslim. (IHRC, 2019)

Muslim Americans experience demonstrations in different venues, but perceive the attitudes and actions directed against them as being a function of their identity. 30.7% of Muslims polled in the survey claim they had experienced educational discrimination due to their religion, while 27% say they experienced job discrimination for the same reason. As to taking action to report the discrimination at work or in their employment, 37.7% claimed that despite their experience of discrimination, they did not lodge a complaint, while 27.7% who had an experience said they were too afraid to report it. 65% of Muslim Americans surveyed see policies and practices, at work or at school, as negatively affecting Muslims. Nearly half (47.1%) have had their religious beliefs challenged by work colleagues, schoolmates and teachers or college peers.

Muslim Americans have without doubt been recipients of hate speech, hate crimes and hate policies, especially over the past two decades. At the same time, however, they remain very optimistic that attitudes toward them and Islam would improve if people had greater personal contact with Muslims. In the SMEHHD, 83.9% of Muslims stated that if people knew more about Muslims, they would act much better than the way they currently do. This sentiment is buttressed by several polls that indicate most Americans have never met, let alone know, a Muslim. Such studies also show that there is a direct correlation between interpersonal relations with Muslims and positive perceptions of Muslims and Islam.

It is therefore imperative for Muslim Americans to develop stronger modes of civic engagement. This can be achieved at the grassroots level even with one's neighbors, schoolmates and work colleagues. The multiplier effect that such interactions can have in their ability to project positive sentiment about the community as a whole is immeasurable. Muslim Americans are already very well integrated into the broader societal fabric. They serve in a variety of service-related occupations, and most Americans probably don't realize that their physician, teacher, bank teller, attorney, pharmacist, retail assistant or first responder is a Muslim.

Non-Muslim communities have demonstrated themselves to be allies when they express solidarity with Muslim Americans to protest and oppose Islamophobia and policies that target Muslims. Employers, schools and other entities that cultivate social engagement can further encourage interaction with Muslims by creating socialization opportunities that do not include and enfranchise Muslims. Oftentimes, "group" functions and activities sponsored by such entities, for example, involve alcohol or venues where alcohol is a key component. This rather arbitrary prerequisite for engagement can be modified and/or replaced by programming that provides for the largest potential capacity of participation, while allowing for greater interaction with Muslim colleagues.

Interpersonal contact is the most effective antidote to negative imagery and rhetoric about Muslims. People have a far greater likelihood of trusting situations in which they have agency over the matter. Interacting with a Muslim American will offer a far more authentic and reliable measure of what Islam or Muslims are like than a third party statement or media report. American society encourages openness and engagement, in general. Muslim Americans need to recognize that the process of rehumanizing and renormalizing Muslims into the broader American social landscape is a critical imperative, and independent of debates they may be having about assimilation. At the same time, Muslim Americans should not be saddled with the burden of persuading people to consider them as human. Rather, there need to be mechanisms that facilitate proving or reminding others of the obvious.

Bibliography

Aghajanian, L. (2017) "What It's Like to Live in Hamtramck, a Majority-Muslim City in Michigan, Right Now." [Online] Available in: https://www.teenvogue.com/story/hamtramck-michigan-majority-muslim-city.

Ahmed-Ullah, N and Cohen, L. (2003) "Two with Chicago Ties Linked to Terrorism." [Online] Available In: https://www.chicagotribune.com/news/ct-xpm-2003-02-21-0302210383-story.html.

Ali, W. (2011). Exposing the Islamophobia Network in America. The Huffington Post. August 29. March 13. Retrieved at 3 April 2020, available online from: http://www.huffingtonpost.com/wajahat-ali/exposing-the-islamophobia_b_938777.html

Alsultany, E. (2015). Muslims are facing a civil rights crisis in America, and it's the media's fault. The Washington Post. November 11. March 13. Retrieved at 2 April 2020, available online from: https://www.washingtonpost.com/news/in-theory/wp/2015/11/11/muslims-are-facing-a-civil-rights-crisis-in-america/?utm_term=.761f9b9d4bbe

Ameli, S. R. (2010). *Domination Hate Model of Intercultural Relations (DHMIR)*. Public speech in the Faculty of World Studies at the University of Tehran.

Ameli, S. R. & Merali, A. (2014). *Only Canadian: The Experience of Hate Moderated Differential Citizenship for Muslims*. London: Islamic Human Rights Commission Publication.

Ameli, S. R. & Merali, A. (2015). *Environment of Hate: The New Normal for Muslims in the UK*. London: Islamic Human Rights Commission Publication.

Ameli, S. R., Merali, A., & Shahghasemi, E. (2012). *France and the Hated Society: Muslim Experiences*. London: Islamic Human Rights Commission Publication.

Ameli, S. R., Mohseni Ahooei, E., Shahghasemi, E. & Rahimpour, M. (2011). *Getting the Message: The Recurrence of Hate Crimes in the UK*. London: Islamic Human Rights Commission Publication.

Ameli, S. R.; Merali, A. & Mohseni Ahooei, E. (2013). *Once Upon a Hatred: Anti-Muslim Experiences in the USA*. London: Islamic Human Rights Commission Publication.

American Civil Liberties Union (n.d.) Racial Profiling. March 13. Retrieved at 3 April 2020, available online from: https://www.aclu.org/issues/racial-justice/race-and-criminal-justice/racial-profiling.

American Scientist (2011). Is Race Real? Retrieved at 28 March 2020, available online from: http://www.americanscientist.org/issues/pub/2011/4/is-race-real

Ansari, A. (2007) *Modern Iran, 2nd Edition*. Harlow: Pearson Longman.

Arab American Institute (2015). American Attitudes towards Arabs and Muslims: 2015. Retrieved at 30 March 2020, available online from: http://www.aaiusa.org/american_attitudes_toward_arabs_and_muslims_2015.

Bagby, I. (2001) *The Mosque in America, A National Portrait: A Report from the Mosque Study Project*. Washington DC: Council on American-Islamic Relations.

Basu, M. (2016). 15 years after 9-11, Sikhs still victims of anti-Muslim hate crimes. CNN. September 15. Retrieved at 1 April 2020, available online from: http://www.cnn.com/2016/09/15/us/sikh-hate-crime-victims/.

Bawardi, H. (2014) *The Making of American Americans: From Syrian Nationalism to U.S. Citizenship*. Austin: University of Texas Press.

Bebow, J. (2004) "Iraqi Spy Gets 46 Months in Prison." [Online]

Available In: https://www.chicagotribune.com/news/ct-xpm-2004-04-01-0404010274-story.html.

Beutel, A. and Jankovic, J. (2015) *Strength Through Diversity: Four Cases of Local and State Level Coalition Success*. Washington, DC: ISPU.

Beutel, A. and Khan, S. (2014) *Manufacturing Bigotry: A State-By-State Legislative Effort to Pushback Against 2050 by Targeting Muslims and Other Minorities*. Washington, DC: ISPU.

BlackPast (2010). (1849) Charles Sumner, Equality before the Law: Unconstitutionality of Separate Colored Schools in Massachusetts. Retrieved 21 April 2020 [online] at: https://www.blackpast.org/african-american-history/1849-charles-sumner-equality-law-unconstitutionality-separate-colored-schools-massachusetts-2/.

Brace, L. (2000). Does Race Exist? Public Broadcasting Service. November 20. Retrieved at 27 March 2020, available online from: http://www.pbs.org/wgbh/nova/evolution/does-race-exist.html

Bronson, R. (2008) *Thicker than Oil: America's Uneasy Partnership with Saudi Arabia*. New York: Oxford University Press.

Cainkar, L. (2009) *Homeland Insecurity*. New York: Russell Sage Foundation.

Carr, J. & Haynes, A. (2015). A clash of racializations: The policing of "race" and of anti-Muslim racism in Ireland. *Critical Sociology*, 41: 21–40.

CBSChicago (2019) "Muslim Family Targeted By Racist, Homophobic Vandalism; Slurs Sprayed On Home, Brick Thrown Through Window." [Online] Available in: https://chicago.cbslocal.com/2019/05/03/bolingbrook-muslim-family-hate-crime-graffiti-brick-through-window/

Chalabi, M. (2015). How anti-Muslim are Americans? Data points to extent of Islamophobia. The Guardian. December 8. Retrieved

at 31 March 2020, available online from:
https://www.theguardian.com/us-news/2015/dec/08/muslims-us-islam-islamophobia-data-polls.
Chu, A. (2015). Targeting for "looking Muslim": The Dawkins/Harris worldview and a twisted new hypocrisy which feeds racism. Salon. March 12. Retrieved at 1 April 2020, available online from:
http://www.salon.com/2015/03/12/targeted_for_looking_muslim_the_dawkinsharris_worldview_and_a_twisted_new_hypocrisy_which_feeds_racism/.

Council on American-Islamic Relations (CAIR) (2016). Confront Fear: Islamophobia and its Impact in the United States (2016 Report). Washington: Council on American-Islamic Relations. Council on American-Islamic Relations (CAIR) (2017). The Empowerment of Hate: The Civil Rights Implications of Islamophobic Bias in the U.S. 2014–2016. Retrieved at 29 March 2020, available online from: http://www.islamophobia.org/15-reports/188-the-empowerment-of-hate.html.

Crawford, T. (2018) "Palestinian Activist Deported to Jordan from Chicago." [Online] Available in:
https://www.chicagotribune.com/news/breaking/ct-palestinian-activist-deported-chicago-20170919-story.html

Curtis, E. (2010) *Encyclopedia of Muslim-American History*. New York: Infobase Publishing.

— (2013) *The Black Muslim Scare of the Twentieth Century: The History of State Islamophobia and its Post-9/11 Variation*. In Ernst, K. (ed.) *Islamophobia in America*. New York: Palgrave MacMillan.

Danner, C. (2016). Flight Delayed, Economist Questioned After Doing Math While Looking Middle Eastern. New York Magazine. May 7. Retrieved at 31 March 2020, available online from:
http://nymag.com/daily/intelligencer/2016/05/economist-profiled-after-doing-math-on-plane.html.

DiBenedetto, S. (2015) "Lake of the Hills Mosque Receives Threatening Letter." [Online] Available in:
https://www.nwherald.com/2015/02/22/lake-in-the-hills-mosque-receives-threatening-letter/adcdeq3/.

DuBois, W. (1903) *The Souls of Black Folk*. Chicago: A.C. McClurgh & Co.

Dunn, K. M.; Klocker, N. & Salabay, T. (2007). Contemporary racism and Islamophobia in Australia: Racializing religion. *Ethnicities, 7*: 564–89.

Ehrlich, H. (1990). *Ethno-Violence on College Campuses*, Baltimore: National Institute against Prejudice and Violence.

Etzioni, A. (2005) *How Patriotic is the Patriot Act?* New York: Routledge.

Fisk, R. (2007) *The Great War for Civilization*. New York: Vintage Books.

Fitzpatrick, M. (2019) *Uncertain Future: The JCPOA and Iran's Nuclear and Missile Programmes*. London: IISS.

Frankenberg, E. (2019). What school segregation looks like in the US today, in 4 charts. Retrieved in Washington Post 29 March 2020 online from http://theconversation.com/what-school-segregation-looks-like-in-the-us-today-in-4-charts-120061.

Gajanan, M. (2018) *Ilhan Omar and Rashida Tlaib Just Became the First Muslim Women Elected to Congress*. [Online] Available in: https://time.com/5445303/ilhan-omar-rashida-tlaib-midterm/.

GALLUP (n.d.). Islamophobia: Understanding Anti-Muslim Sentiment in the West. Retrieved in Washington Post 29 March 2020 online from https://news.gallup.com/poll/157082/islamophobia-understanding-anti-muslim-sentiment-west.aspx.

GhaneaBassiri, K. (2010) *A History of Islam in America*. New York: Cambridge University Press.

Graham, D. (2015) *Why the Muslim 'No-Go-Zone' Myth Won't Die*. [online] Available in: https://www.theatlantic.com/international/archive/2015/01/paris-mayor-to-sue-fox-over-no-go-zone-comments/384656/

Graham, R. (2016) *"The Professor Wore a Hijab in Solidarity — Then Lost Her Job."* [Online] Available in: https://www.nytimes.com/2016/10/16/magazine/the-professor-wore-a-hijab-in-solidarity-then-lost-her-job.html.

Greenwald, G. and Hussain, M. (2014) *Meet the Muslim Americans the NSA and FBI Have Been Spying On.* [Online] Available at https://theintercept.com/2014/07/09/under-surveillance/.

Grosfoguel, R. (2010) "Epistemic Islamophobia and Colonial Social Sciences." *Human Architecture: Journal of the Sociology of Self-Knowledge.* 8:2, 29-38.

Grynbaum, M. and Otterman, S. (2015) *New York City Adds 2 Muslim Holy Days to Public School Calendar.* [Online] Available in: https://www.nytimes.com/2015/03/05/nyregion/new-york-to-add-two-muslim-holy-days-to-public-school-calendar.html.

Hafiz, Y. (2014) "Terry Jones, Quran-Burning Pastor, Plans 'Dearborn Freedom Rally' In Front Of Mosque." [Online] Available In: https://www.huffpost.com/entry/terry-jones-dearborn-freedom-rally_n_5433994.

Herrick, D. (2018) *Esteban: The African Slave Who Explored America.* Albuquerque: University of New Mexico Press.

Howell, S. (2014) *Old Islam in Detroit.* New York: Oxford University Press.

Kar, D. (2010) *U.S. Dept. of Justice Supports Tenn. Mosque in Brief.* Washington, DC: Muslim Advocates. [Online] Available at https://muslimadvocates.org/2010/09/u-s-dept-of-justice-supports-tenn-mosque-in-brief/.

Kearns, E. M.; Betus, A. & Lemieux. A. (2017a). Why Do Some Terrorist Attacks Receive More Media Attention Than Others. Social Science Research Network. March 7. March 13. Retrieved at 1 April 2020, available online from: https://papers.ssrn.com/sol3/papers.cfm?abstract_id=2928138.

Kearns, E. M.; Betus, A. & Lemieux. A. (2017b). Yes, the media do underreport some terrorist attacks. Just not the ones most people think of. The Washington Post. March 13. Retrieved at 1 April 2020, available online from: https://www.washingtonpost.com/news/monkey-cage/wp/2017/03/13/yes-the-media-do-underreport-some-te rrorist-attacks-just-not-the-ones-most-people-think-of/?utm_term=.88d3b539de96.

Keeter, S. (2007) *Muslim Americans: Middle Class and Mostly Mainstream*. Pew Research Center.

Khalid, M. (2011). Gender, orientalism and representations of the "Other" in the War on Terror. *Global Change, Peace & Security, 23*: 15–29.

Khan, S. and Siddiqui, S. (2017) *Islamic Education in the United States and the Evolution of Muslim Nonprofit Institutions*. Cheltenham: Edward Elgar Publishing.

Kinzer, S. (2003) *All the Shah's Men*. Hoboken: John Wiley & Sons.

Kundnani, A. (2014) *The Muslims are Coming!: Islamophobia, Extremism, and the Domestic War on Terror*. London: Verso Books.

Kuruvilla, C. (2019) *"'Islamophobe' Pastor's Church Cancels Anti-Muslim Lecture Series After Backlash."* [Online] Available in: https://www.huffpost.com/entry/bloomfield-hills-baptist-church_n_5d790b8ee4b0a938a42be023

Lean, N. (2012).*The Islamophobia Industry: How the Right Manufactures Fear of Muslims*. London: Pluto Press.

Levin, B. (2016). Special Status Report: Hate Crime in the United States (20 State Compilation of Official Data). San Bernardino: Center for the Study of Hate & Extremism at the California State University, Retrieved at 29 March 2020, available online from: https://www.documentcloud.org/documents/3110202-SPECIAL-STATUS-REPORT-v5-9-16-16.html.

Levin, J. & McDevitt, J. (1993). *Hate crimes. The Rising Tide of Bigotry and Bloodshed*, New York and London: Plenum Press.

Lichtblau, E. (2016). Hate Crimes against American Muslims Most since Post-9/11 Era. The New York Times. September 17. Retrieved at 30 March 2020, available online from: https://www.nytimes.com/2016/09/18/us/politics/hate-crimes-american-muslims-rise.html.

Longman, J. (2011) *All-Nighters for a Football Team During Ramadan.* [Online] Available in: https://www.nytimes.com/2011/08/11/sports/football/all-nighters-keep-football-team-competitive-during-ramadan.html.

Love, E. (2017) *Islamophobia and Racism in America.* New York: New York University Press.

McGhee, J. (2019) "Chicago Lieutenant Among Hundreds of Cops to Post Hateful Comments on Facebook." [Online] Available in: https://www.chicagoreporter.com/chicago-lieutenant-with-history-of-complaints-among-hundreds-of-cops-to-post-hateful-comments-on-facebook/.

Media Tenor International (2011). *A New Era for Arab-Western Relations - Media analysis.* New York: Media Tenor.

Meer, N. & Modood, T. (2009). Refutations of racism in the "Muslim question". *Patterns of Prejudice, 43*: 335–54.

Mellnik, T.; Cameron, D.; Lu, D.; Badger, E. & Downs, K. (2016). America's great housing divide: Are you a winner or loser? Retrieved in Washington Post 29 March 2020 online from: https://www.washingtonpost.com/graphics/business/wonk/housing/overview/.

Misra, T. (2018) "When Your Block is Being Watched." [Online] Available in: https://www.citylab.com/equity/2018/10/when-your-block-being-watched/573157/

Naidoo, K. (2016). The origins of hate-crime laws. *Fundamina.* 22(1): 53-66.

Narea, N. (2020) "Nearly 200 Iranian Americans Were Detained at the US-Canada Border." [Online] Available In: https://www.vox.com/2020/1/7/21054780/iran-trump-detain-canada-border-soleimani.

Nawaz, S. (2008) *Crossed Swords: Pakistan, its Army, and the Wars Within*. Oxford: Oxford University Press.

Omi, M. & Winant, H. (1994). *Racial Formation in the United States: From the 1960s to the 1990s*. New York and London: Routledge.

Pew Research Center. (2007) *Muslim Americans: Middle Class and Mostly Mainstream*. Washington, DC: Pew Research Center.

—— (2014). How Americans Feel About Religious Groups. The Pew Forum. July 16. Retrieved at 30 March 2020, available online from: http://www.pewforum.org/2014/07/16/how-americans-feel-about-religious-groups/.

—— (2017) New Estimates Show U.S. Muslim Population Continues to Grow. [Online] Available in: https://www.pewresearch.org/fact-tank/2018/01/03/new-estimates-show-u-s-muslim-population-continues-to-grow/

Poynting, S. & Mason, V. (2006). Tolerance, freedom, justice and peace? Britain, Australia, and anti-Muslim racism since 11 September 2001. *Journal of Intercultural Studies*, 27: 61–86.

Puskar, S. (2007) *Bosnian Muslims of Chicagoland*. Charleston: Arcadia Publishing.

Rosenberg, Y. (2019) The Complicated History of Jefferson's Koran. [Online] Available in: https://www.washingtonpost.com/outlook/2019/01/02/complicated-history-thomas-jeffersons-koran/.

Runnymede Trust (1997). Islamophobia: A challenge for us all. The Runnymede Trust. Retrieved at 28 March 2020, available online from: http://www.runnymedetrust.org/uploads/publications/pdfs/islamophobia.pdf.

Samari, G. (2016). Islamophobia and public health in the United States. *American Journal of Public Health, 106*: 1920–5.

Sayigh, Y. and Shlaim, A. (2003) *The Cold War and the Middle East.* Oxford: Oxford University Press.

Shaheen, J.G. (2012). *Reel Bad Arabs: How Hollywood Vilifies a People (Revised and updated ed.).* New York: Olive Branch Press, Interlink Publishing Group.

Siddiqui, S. (2014). Americans' Attitudes toward Muslims and Arabs Are Getting Worse, Poll Finds. The Huffington Post. July 29. Retrieved at 30 March 2020, available online from: http://www.huffingtonpost.com/2014/07/29/arab-muslim-poll_n_5628919.html.

Sikh Coalition (2012). Statement for the Record from the Sikh Coalition. The Sikh Coalition. September 19 Retrieved at 1 April 2020, available online from: http://www.sikhcoalition.org/images/documents/statementfort herecordfromthesikhcoalition.pdf.

Sikh Coalition (2015). FBI Finally Recognizes Sikhs in New Hate Crime Tracking Program. The Sikh Coalition. March 25. Retrieved at 2 April 2020, available online from: http://www.sikhcoalition.org/advisories/2015/fbi-finally-recognizes-sikhs-in-new-hate-crime-tracking-program.

Smith, J. (1999) *Islam in America.* Columbia University Press.

Southern Poverty Law Center (2020) *Tracking Anti-Muslim Legislation Across the U.S.* [Online] Available in: https://www.splcenter.org/data-projects/tracking-anti-muslim-legislation-across-us.

State of Oklahoma (2010) Oklahoma International and Sharia Law, State Question 755.

Streissguth, T. (2003). *Hate Crimes* (Library in a Book). Facts on File.

Sweeney, A. (2019) "Muslim Community Leader Throws Out First Pitch at Cubs Game as Team Continues Outreach." [Online] Available in: https://www.chicagotribune.com/news/ct-muslim-leader-first-pitch-cubs-20190716-b2jfh2xi7vea5kowzqlh5schae-story.html.

Tal, D. (2019) *US Strategic Arms Policy in the Cold War: Negotiation and Confrontation Over SALT, 1969-1979.* Abingdon: Routledge.

Telhami, S. (2015). What Americans really think about Muslims and Islam? The Brookings Institution. December 9. March 13. Retrieved at 3 April 2020, available online from: https://www.brookings.edu/blog/markaz/2015/12/09/what-americans-really-think-about-muslims-and-islam/.

Uddin, A. (2014) *Religious Freedom and Discrimination in America – Then and Now: Lessons Learned for American Muslims and Their Allies.* Washington, DC: ISPU.

United States. (1969) *Civil Rights Acts of 1957, 1960, 1964, 1968, and Voting Rights Act of 1965.* Washington: U.S. GPO.

—— (1980) *Immigration and Nationality Act, with Amendments and Notes on Related Laws.* Washington :U.S. G.P.O.

—— (1988) *The Kerner Report: The 1968 Report of the National Advisory Commission on Civil Disorders.*

—— (2000) *The Religious Land Use and Institutionalized Persons Act,* Pub.L. 106–274, codified as 42 U.S.C. § 2000cc et seq.

—— (2001) *The USA PATRIOT Act: Preserving Life and Liberty : Uniting and Ptrengthening America by Providing Appropriate Tools Required to Intercept and Obstruct Terrorism.* Washington, D.C.: U.S. Dept. of Justice.

—— (2012) *The U.S. Constitution.* Naperville: Oak Hill Publishing.

Warikoo, N. (2019) "Muslim Candidates in Michigan Faced Hate During Political Campaigns in 2018." [Online] Available in: https://www.freep.com/story/news/local/michigan/2019/11/

10/muslim-candidates-faced-hate-michigan-2018-elections/2525982001/.

—— (2017) "Michigan Man Linked to ISIS Sentenced to Five Years." [Online] Available in: https://www.usatoday.com/story/news/nation/2013/04/29/arab-festival-moved-religious-tensions/2120233/.

—— (2013) "Michigan Arab Festival Moved After Religious Tensions." [Online] Available in: https://www.xfinity.com/stream/live/Watch-Parental Guidance/5956076898283714105/POP.

Wilkins, K. G. (2008). *Home/Land/Security: What We Learn About Arab Communities from Action-Adventure Films*. Lanham: Row man & Littlefield.

Williams, A. & Emam djomeh, A. (2018). America is more diverse than ever — but still segregated. Retrieved in Washington Post 29 March 2020 online from https://www.washingtonpost.com/graphics/2018/national/segregation-us-cities/.

Yglesias, M. (2019) *Trump's Racist Tirades Against "the Squad" Explained*. [Online] Available in: https://www.vox.com/2019/7/15/20694616/donald-trump-racist-tweets-omar-aoc-tlaib-pressley.